From the Needle to the Cross

A Journey Through Tragedy to Triumph

Abundant Life!
John 10:10

Amanda S
2022

By Amanda Sexton

TRILOGY

Trilogy Christian Publishers
A Wholly Owned Subsidiary of Trinity Broadcasting Network
2442 Michelle Drive
Tustin, CA 92780
Copyright © 2021 by **Amanda Sexton**
All Scripture quotations, unless otherwise noted, taken from THE HOLY BIBLE, NEW KING JAMES VERSION®, NKJV® Copyright © 1973, 1978, 1984, 2011 by Biblica, Inc.® Used by permission. All rights reserved worldwide.
Scripture quotations marked (KJV) taken from The Holy Bible, King James Version. Cambridge Edition: 1769.
All rights reserved, including the right to reproduce this book or portions thereof in any form whatsoever.
For information, address Trilogy Christian Publishing
Rights Department, 2442 Michelle Drive, Tustin, Ca 92780.
First Trilogy Christian Publishing hardcover edition May 2018
Trilogy Christian Publishing/ TBN and colophon are trademarks of Trinity Broadcasting Network.
For information about special discounts for bulk purchases, please contact Trilogy Christian Publishing.
Manufactured in the United States of America

10 9 8 7 6 5 4 3 2 1
Library of Congress Cataloging-in-Publication Data is available.
ISBN 978-1-68556-024-9
ISBN 978-1-68556-025-6 (ebook)

DEDICATION

I dedicate this book to my husband, Jamie Sexton, for walking this journey with me and never giving up on me, even when I wanted to give up on myself. I love you.

Acknowledgements

There are so many people I would like to thank for all their help in writing this book as well as helping me in my walk with Christ and through recovery to get to the place where I could even begin to write this book, let alone finish it, that I do not really know where to start and could write an entire novel if I listed you all by name. Know that I love you all and am extremely thankful for each of you!

So here goes with the list... First and foremost, I have to thank God. It is only by His grace that I am even still standing, let alone writing and going forward for the glory of the Lord. I am also so grateful to have such wonderful and loving parents. My mom and dad, Becky and Bill Simmons, who have gone on to be with Jesus, and my God-given mother, Jannie Simmons, who is still walking this thing out with me day by day. I do not want to even think about where I would be if it were not for their love, prayers, and support.

My husband, Jamie Sexton, is most definitely my knight in shining armor, the rock that Christ intended for husbands to be. Evan and Caleb Sexton, my sons, the very apples of my eye. I love them so very much.

I'm forever grateful to have such wonderful spiritual parents, Dr. Frank and Karen Sumrall. They are so wonderful and tell me what I need to hear, not only what I want to hear, and give me clear direction from the Lord. My sponsor, Donna Skeens, who has always been right there and willing to give me the hard truth along with her husband, Lonnie, who may be the softer, easier side. He is usually the more loving one when she would give me the *what for* so to speak. I also want to thank Pastors Wade and Denise McGeorge for their support and encouragement in writing this book and allowing God to use them in many ways in my life. One of which was God speaking the title of the book to Pastor Denise as she laid her hand on the manuscript.

I have to give special thanks and all kinds of kudos to my cousin, Donna Brown Wilkerson, who worked endless hours to help me with this book. She not only helped with editing and critiquing, but she pushed me to open up and allow myself to be vulnerable in ways I did not think I ever could. For this, I am forever grateful. I love you all, and I am so very thankful God placed each of you in my life, as well as all my friends, family members, and spiritual family members who have spurred me forward. Last but most definitely not least, thank you, Trilogy Publishing. I have extreme gratitude toward each and every individual on the team for making the publishing process easier than expected.

Table of Contents

Foreword 09
Introduction 13

Chapter 1: How Did I Get Here?........................15
Chapter 2: Where it All Began........................27
Chapter 3: The Effects of Divorce....................41
Chapter 4: Me and Momma..............................49
Chapter 5: My Dysfunctional Family Tree..........57
Chapter 6: Sex, Drugs, & Rock n' Roll.............71
Chapter 7: On the Hunt...............................79
Chapter 8: Momma's Sick & I'm out of Control...87
Chapter 9: I Said, "No!".............................97
Chapter 10: When Suicide Becomes an Option...103
Chapter 11: Long History of Abuse................107
Chapter 12: Battered & Bruised.....................115
Chapter 13: My Senior Year.........................123
Chapter 14: The Needle..............................133
Chapter 15: Rejection...............................147
Chapter 16: Get help................................155
Chapter 17: A Second Chance.......................165
Chapter 18: Hanging on by a Thread...............177
Chapter 19: Lying, Cheating, & Stealing..........187

CHAPTER 20: TOTAL LOSS OF SELF CONTROL..........197
CHAPTER 21: DEATH..205
CHAPTER 22: CLOSE CALL................................215
CHAPTER 23: SELFISHNESS...............................225
CHAPTER 24: BOTTOM.....................................235
CHAPTER 25: DIVINE PROTECTION.....................247
CHAPTER 26: AMAZING GRACE.........................261
CHAPTER 27: THE ABUNDANT LIFE......................271

EPILOGUE   277

Foreword

To appoint unto them that mourn in Zion, to give unto them beauty for ashes, the oil of joy for mourning, the garment of praise for the spirit of heaviness; that they might be called trees of righteousness, the planting of the lord, that he might be glorified.

Isaiah 61:3

As Amanda walks her readers through her long dark journey, she weaves a plot of Satan's strategy to destroy her and the generations before her and behind her. The story of her darkest nights as the one in the cow pasture will be a divine testimony of those who sit in darkness that receive a marvelous light revelation; of our Father's God divine love for us (Matthew 4). His rescuing power that is unrelenting to those He loves!

Amanda's darkness of night from her birth and her bloodline will reveal the cruelest and demonic schemes of addictions that have tentacles reaching generations before and after, if not broken by the precious blood of Jesus!

Science calls it hereditary, while those of us who study God's Word reveals these strongholds as the chains of Satan for eternity, if not broken and destroyed from the roots. Only the saving love of Jesus and His blood on the cross can leave a trail of the links of those chains in the dust!

This author will take you on a trail of the enemy's lies and deceit for years that paint a picture of the darkness and dysfunction in the lives of those she loves and the details of those born before her.

Here we find sin plotting a spider web of lies, cheating, alcoholics, drug addicts, sexual perversion, and incest that has destroyed the lives of many and sent many into premature deaths to their bodies and souls and early graves! Without the saving grace of God, where would many of us be?

From the Needle to the Cross will help many to understand their own lives and pull the curtains up to reveal the tragedies of a lost soul who wallowed in that cow mud that long-ago night, to be a mighty and powerful voice in her generation and those to come! She sets the stage with a helping hand from our beloved Holy Spirit; to lean down her hand and pull all those lying in darkness to the glorious light of Jesus! She loudly proclaims how He did it for her, and He will do it for you! Our Lord Jesus is no respecter of persons; He loves you as He loves her.

We are so proud of Amanda. We ordained her husband, Jaime & her, for the kingdom of God. We have watched them grow more and more in love for Jesus as the years pass, and now they carry that same resurrection power of Jesus that He arose with that third day. Many need that third-day resurrection power today and what they carry. They are bold for the Gospel of Jesus and spend every waking moment to rescue all those that cross their paths with the same power!

"Therefore I say to you, her sins, which are many, are forgiven, for she loved much. But to whom little is forgiven, *the same* loves little" (Luke 7:47).

We recommend this book and endorse it with our love to all who need Jesus in their darkest of nights. Let Amanda's story for His glory help you up out of the miry mud today and lead you to the light of Jesus's love for you! Believe in His love and plan for your life. He will turn your ashes for beauty too!

Lovingly,

Dr. Frank & Karen Sumrall
Sumrallglobalministries.com

Introduction

I have written this book as a true account of my life, what I have been through and how God has brought me out of a life consumed by addiction. My purpose and prayer for this book are to give anyone struggling with addiction the hope of knowing they are not alone and that they can escape. I also want the families and loved ones of those struggling with addiction to know there is hope of deliverance for their loved ones. Don't give up, and don't quit praying! Miracles do still happen today. I am living proof. Jesus still saves, delivers, and heals.

Although the following is a true story, some names have been changed to protect the privacy and identity of others.

Chapter One

How Did I Get Here?

On a cold and wet October night in 2004, I found myself hiding under a pile of logs in a cow pasture and praying to God to get me out of the mess I had made for myself. I was twenty-three years old, I was scared, and I felt hopeless. Although I desperately wanted out of the situation I was in, I had no idea how to make that happen. I was on the run from the police and terrified of going to jail. My fear of incarceration was not because I cared about my reputation, my freedom, or even my future; it was because if I was in jail, I would no longer have access to drugs. That's just the honest truth. Drugs were my life. They were all that I knew. Drugs had become my god, my lover, my best friend, my comforter, my everything. I didn't think I could survive without drugs, so I did everything in my power to avoid being arrested.

Earlier in the evening, I had been hanging out with my friend, John, getting high on "meth," which is short for crystal methamphetamine, a potent, highly addictive, and illegal street drug. Meth was just one of many drugs that I took during my teens and early twenties, but, at the time, it was my drug of choice. There were warrants out for my arrest, but because John and I had chosen to party a county over from my hometown, I had felt fairly safe. The local cops in that county didn't know me like they did back home. Unfortunately, my extended family and I were well-known (and not for good reasons, but more on that later) in the small Tennessee mountaintop town in which I had grown up.

I didn't know John all that well, but he seemed like a good enough guy. He was quite a bit older than me and looked out for me. Somehow, he made me feel safe, almost like a father figure would have. That feeling of protection was something I desperately craved, although I couldn't have verbalized that at the time.

John and I had been up for quite some time and had been doing drugs for several days at that point. I was too messed up to know or even care about the details, but I do remember that we had been going at it pretty hard and heavy. We were really high and wired up. Strange as it may sound, despite me being wanted by the law in another county, we were just out partying and getting high without a care in the world. I never even thought about getting busted that night. In fact, we had chosen to go to that specific county for the very reason that there were rarely any law enforcement officers to be seen there. I had partied in that same place many times over the years and never even seen a patrol car.

So, there we were, just driving along without a care in the world (not to mention high as a kite), and what do we see but blue lights in the rear-view mirror. John knew my situation. He knew I was wanted. He looked at me and said, "What do you want to do?" I told him it was up to him. Even in my drug-induced state, I didn't want to see him get in trouble. I knew it was his vehicle, and they had already run his tags and knew who the vehicle belonged to. We didn't have enough drugs or paraphernalia on us at that particular time for John himself to have gotten into any major trouble, but he still chose to run in order to keep me from going to jail. He floored it, and I just held on.

I don't know how long the chase lasted. It seemed like just seconds because of all the adrenaline, meth, and who knows what else that was pumping through my veins. In reality, however, I know that it was much longer because of the distance that we covered, also, by the time that we turned down an old dirt road—which had become extremely muddy road due to all the rain. Our unwelcome visitor had friends, so now there was not just one officer but several cop cars following closely behind, us all with their blue lights flashing and their sirens wailing. The one advantage that we had was that we were in a four-wheel-drive sport utility vehicle, while the officers were in regular police cruisers. The SUV proved to be much more maneuverable on the muddy backroads than the police cars, and we were finally able to get some distance between them and us—until we hit the creek, that is. The creek covered the entire width of the road, and we had no choice but to drive straight into it. When that happened, we were stuck, and as they say in the South, "marred up" and not going anywhere. In the few minutes before the cops caught up with us, John looked me in the eye and shouted at me to run. We opened the doors of the SUV and ran as hard and fast as we could in opposite directions.

I won't lie and try to act tough. I was scared. I had run from the local police in my hometown after some Halloween mischief a few times and had managed to evade being pulled over while driving once or twice, but I had never done anything like this before. To leave the SUV and flee on foot into the dark Tennessee night was a whole new ballgame. The pitch-black dark, the effects of the drugs, and the sheer exhaustion from having been up for several days all added to my uncertainty and panic.

Almost immediately, one of my shoes got stuck in the mud. Now, not only was the vehicle marred up in the mud, but I was, too, not just physically but also spiritually, mentally, and emotionally. I was wearing old brown leather clogs that night, one of my favorite pairs of shoes, actually. I loved those clogs. That style was coming back in at the time, the worn-out hippie look. Despite my momentary frustration and sense of loss, I knew I was going to have to leave the clogs behind if I was going to make it. I slipped my foot out of the one that stuck in the mud, kicked the other one off, and took off running in my sock feet.

I ran up a hill on the side of the creek, continuing until I came to a fence that enclosed a cow pasture. In hindsight, stumbling along that disgusting minefield of cow patties in sock feet should have upset me more than the shoe situation, but the thought never crossed my mind. My only concern was to get as far away from the police—and the possibility of detoxing from meth in the county jail—as possible.

I was midway through that soggy, stinky field when I heard the police catch up to our then-abandoned vehicle. I froze, caught in a panic until I saw my refuge, a pile of old logs in the middle of the cow pasture. I ran to the logs as fast as I could. Because of the way that they were positioned, I was able to crawl up under them and hide from the officers that I knew would be arriving soon. The ground was wet and cold, and I was shivering and shaking, not just from the physical how caught my attention. My first thought was that if I could get into the car, I might be able to at least warm up a little. By that point, I was soaking wet and freezing from trudging through the creek where we had gotten stuck and then lying in that cold, wet cow pasture for who knows how long. I walked over to the car and tried opening the door. Surprisingly, it was unlocked, so I got in and sat there for a few minutes, shaking and shivering. As I began to warm up a bit, I noticed that there were clothes and shoes in the car. Then, I realized that the keys were in the ignition.

You may be thinking, *Uh-oh,* and you are right—uh-oh. I was about to do one of the stupidest things I have ever done in my entire life.

To my credit, I did sit there for a few more minutes looking at the keys, then looking at the clothes and shoes, then back at the keys, and so on. I was muddy. I was dripping wet. I was freezing. Also, did I mention that I was still hopped up on meth and exercising the extremely poor judgment of someone who had been up for several days and was extremely desperate to avoid going to jail because that would have put a major obstacle between me and my next high? As the saying goes, "Desperate times call for desperate measures."

I fumbled through the clothes that were in the car and found a sweatshirt and a pair of sweatpants. I thought to myself, *I'll just try them on.* Yeah, right! They actually fit me, a little baggy, but they fit. Amazingly, I then tried on a pair of tennis shoes that were on the floorboard on the passenger side, and, voila, they fit too! It was almost as if I had stumbled onto the belongings of a sober, cleaner, more well-fed version of myself.

After I put the dry clothes and shoes on, I sat there for a few more minutes, warming up and trying to decide what to do. I looked at the keys, then looked at the door of the house, then looked at the keys, then looked at the door of the house. Eventually, curiosity got the best of me. I thought, *Surely this car doesn't run. I'm sure that's why they left the keys in it.* Wrong! I turned the key over, and it started right up! I still sat there for a few more minutes, somewhat in shock and not really knowing what to do because I had never taken anyone else's vehicle. I actually had not intended on taking *that* vehicle when I first got into it (nor had I thought of stealing any vehicle, ever, for that matter). That was not my desire, nor my intention. My only thoughts were of getting out of there at that time. I looked at the door of the house for a few more minutes, thinking someone would surely come out and see me. No one did. So, I took off.

I didn't "peel out" or anything like that. I drove normally. I just wanted to get home, to be away from that place and that nightmare of a night—and, truth be told, that nightmare of a life to finally be over. I had another problem, however. I was lost, not just spiritually but literally. Because of the slapdash manner in which we had run from the cops, I didn't have a clue where I was. Keep in mind that things like smartphones and in-dash navigators were still a few years away. It was just me and my instincts.

I just kept driving until I finally came to a place that was familiar to me. I then headed toward the interstate and drove toward my hometown. As I started to get off on my exit, the car died suddenly. Looking back, I believe the car died exactly where it needed to because even though I had only taken the car out of desperation and originally had no plans as to what I would do with it when I got to where I was going, on the drive I was already starting to think of how I could trade the car for dope.

The addict mind had already started to kick in, take over, and take the matter to a whole other level. I wasn't a career criminal. I didn't steal cars for a living. I had simply been fortunate to have found that particular car (and clothes and shoes) to help me out of a desperate situation. In the time that it had taken me to drive from one county to another, however, the wheels had already begun to turn in my mind as to how the blessing of the car could be turned around and used for the sin of more drug use. God knew this, of course, and I believe that He began to intervene at this point because of the prayer I had just prayed in that cow pasture.

I left the car parked where it died and took off walking. It was almost daylight by this time, so I was starting to get scared again. I had some fear while driving the car, but mainly I was intently focused on the fact that I was getting out of that terrible situation and going home. The possible legal ramifications of what I was doing were not fully computing at the time. I'm not sure if it was due to all the drug use, the fact that I was not actually seeing blue lights at the moment, or the fact that I had finally prayed a sincere prayer to the One who was coming to rescue me and lead me out of my mess. Maybe it was a combination of all three.

When the fear did hit me after I parked the now-useless stolen car, I knew I couldn't just take off walking down the interstate. I was now in the very county in which I was wanted by the law. I looked around at my surroundings; I needed a plan. I saw a fence on the side of the interstate. On the other side of the fence were homes. I had my plan: jump the fence and get to one of those houses. So, that's exactly what I did. I climbed over the fence. As soon as I tumbled over the fence, I noticed a house in the distance with a light on. I darted straight for that home, went to the door, and knocked. A very nice lady came to the door. I told her my car had broken down and that I needed a ride to my mom's house, just a few miles away. She said she would get her husband, and she did. He then took me to my mom's, where I was finally safe.

I don't remember the couple's names. I wish I did because I would really like to thank them. They were extremely nice to me when I didn't deserve such kindness. I could tell they seemed a little scared when I first came to their door. After all, there I was, a drug addict in oversized clothing with muddy hair and what had to have been a pretty crazed expression on my face. I'm sure that's why the lady said, "Let me get my husband." Still, that man chose to take me home. He even offered to help me with "my" car, but I told him that I just needed to get to my mom's.

I don't remember much about what was said on our way to my mother's house, but I do remember the man telling me that he was a pastor. I don't remember him witnessing to me exactly, but I'm sure he did since I do at least remember that he was a preacher. I was just in such bad shape mentally, emotionally, and physically due to the drug use and my legal situation that I couldn't comprehend much of what was going on. All I knew was that I needed to get to my momma, to somewhere that felt safe and secure.

Now, looking back, I can see how the house where that preacher lived was my beacon of hope. It was my lighthouse. God was illuminating my path. Jesus is my Lighthouse, the One who shows me the way, and He was putting people in my path to show me where I needed to go that night. I'm sure that gentleman and his wife not only helped me get to my mom but that they prayed for me and their prayers were a piece of what led to me eventually encountering the Light of the World, Jesus Christ.

∙ ∙ ∙

Please know that I am not proud of any of this. But for the grace of God, I could never have found my way out of the hell that I was living in, and I would never encourage this kind of behavior in any way. I have told you this story so that you can better understand who I was before I came to know Christ and how I lived my life before accepting Him into my heart.

Unless you have been there yourself, you probably wonder how a twenty-three-year-old girl from a small Southern town could have ended up in a situation like that. I understand. Throughout my recovery, I had to ask myself that same question and face the answer—however painful it was—before I could move forward to the next phase of my life.

Through His grace and mercy, I was able to find the answers that I longed for, overcome my addiction, and dedicate my life to His service. I have a wonderful family now, many loving friends, and a job that allows me to help others who may have lost their way. I hope that my story can be an inspiration to others who are suffering or who have family members in situations similar to the one in which I found myself on that terrible October night back in 2004. There is hope! There can be a happy ending!

Before we get to that, though, I think I need to take you on a journey back to where my story really began.

Chapter Two

Where it All Began

My mom, Becky Allen, ran away from home at seventeen years old in the middle of a horrible snowstorm. She was being physically abused at home by her mother and couldn't take it anymore. It was the middle of her senior year, and she was ranked first in her class academically. She was expected to graduate as valedictorian in just a few short months, but, unfortunately, that was not the way things would turn out for young Becky.

My mom was a very intelligent woman when it came to "book sense," but she was not always so smart in other areas. She had made some mistakes earlier during her senior year, experimenting with drugs and alcohol as so many kids her age did at the time. My grandmother found out about it, came home drunk from a bar, and beat

Momma rather severely. Obviously, there is a great deal of irony in that series of events.

My grandmother had a history of beating my mom, but a beating this severe had not happened in a long time. At one point when she was younger, Becky was actually removed from the home by the State of Tennessee and placed in foster care due to my grandmother's abusive behavior. Eventually, my mom was returned to my grandmother's home, and they got along fairly well for a while.

My mother once told me that she had actually loved the foster home they placed her in. This was partially because she hadn't had her dad in her life since she was very young and had never had a stable father figure in her life, except for the foster dad. He was a professor at Tennessee Technological University. His wife was a wonderful woman and a great foster mom, as well. As most parents would have done under the circumstances, my grandmother did what needed to be done so that my mom could come back home. Despite her cruelties, my grandmother did love my mother on some level, as best she could, given her own personal situation.

Part of Momma wanted to go back to Nanny (my name for my grandmother) because she had a younger brother and a younger sister. My uncle Nick was six years younger than Momma, and my aunt Sissy was seven years younger than her. In truth, my mother was more like a mom to them than a big sister. Because of her being older than them and because my grandmother was gone (or drinking) a lot of the time, Becky had helped raise her siblings. She loved them and had always tried to take care of them as best she could. She knew what might happen to them if she didn't come back to live with my grandmother.

From what others have told me, Momma was not only bright but also a very sweet and outgoing young lady. She was part of her high school cheerleading squad, but she didn't have much of an upbringing and didn't have much support at home. Nanny had an alcohol problem, and, perhaps even worse, she had a boyfriend with an alcohol problem.

My grandfather had died when my mom was nine years old, and my aunt and uncle were still toddlers. He had been convicted of killing a man just a few days before his death—which was recorded as a jailhouse suicide, although some in the family doubted that he truly died at his own hand. In recent years, I have learned that Nanny was actually my grandfather's second wife (or possibly his third) and that his first marriage ended after an incident of domestic abuse against his first wife, who took their two children and left the state, never to return.

Truth be told, my mom's life was not so good when her father was still alive, either. He, too, was an alcoholic and more than likely a drug addict, as well. My grandmother wasn't abusive to my mother when my grandfather was alive, but my grandfather himself was very physically abusive toward my grandmother, and he was abusive toward my mom, Becky, in other ways. His untimely death was both a blessing and a curse. It was difficult for my mom to grow up in a small town where everyone knew the ugly details about who her father was, what he had done, and even how he had died, but what was even more tragic were the happenings very few knew about. My grandfather had been sexually abusing my mother for years. It was not only my grandfather, either. He would also bring another adult male into my mom's bedroom and allow him to sexually abuse my mother, too.

My mom always questioned why my Nanny never said or did anything to prevent or stop this abuse. She questioned if she knew what was going on and, even more so, how she could not have known what was going on. From the outside looking in, I have personally always questioned if this was one of the main reasons my grandmother was so abusive toward my mom and had such ill will toward her. I know she loved her in her own way, but she seemed to also hate her at times. She was very different toward my mom than the other children. Whether this was the result of guilt, jealousy, or something else, I will never know, but I do know that it affected my mother and grandmother's relationship deeply.

I should probably also mention that my grandmother had two older sons by another man before she met my grandfather. When she met my grandfather, he forced her to give the children up in order to stay in a relationship with him. I don't know all the details about this. From what I was told, finances and other family attachments played a part in this decision. No matter the reasoning behind this choice, the guilt of this, too, must have overwhelmed my grandmother at times, especially knowing that the man for whom she left her first children had abused their daughter in unspeakable ways.

Getting back to my mother's story, young Becky Allen had a rough life, to say the least. It is fair to say, however, that the more severe beatings did stop, at least for the most part, after she was returned to my grandmother's home from foster care—that is, until Nanny, my grandmother, found out about Becky's alcohol and drug use. Nanny came home drunk with her boyfriend and beat Becky up pretty badly. At that point, Becky had had enough. Even though she was only seventeen and was just a few months away from graduating from high school as class valedictorian, my mother chose to walk out of her childhood home, away from her mother and siblings, and into the middle of a dangerous snowstorm on a cold winter night. Although she didn't have much of a plan other than getting away (sound familiar?), she walked out of the door with no intentions of looking back. That was the night that she met Bill Simmons, who later became my dad.

Bill was a professional truck driver who had an interesting story himself. He was much, much older than my mom; when they met, she was seventeen, and he was forty-three. His father had been killed in a coal mining accident when my father was just four years old. According to my grandfather's death certificate, he was killed instantly by a slate fall in a coal mine in Red Ash, Virginia, in January 1940 when he was just twenty-eight years old. The accident probably fractured his cervical spine and severed his spinal cord. Tragically, my great-grandfather (my father's grandpa) was also killed in a coal mining accident. He died in 1921 when a rock fell on his head inside the mine, fracturing his skull and dislocating his neck. He was in his early forties.

My father was my grandfather's only child, but my father's mother remarried and had more children with her new husband. Although his stepfather treated Dad well enough, my grandmother didn't always treat him so kindly. Not surprisingly, as soon as my dad could leave home, he did. I was told he lied about his age to enter the Navy. You could get away with that back then. He entered the United States Navy at the age of seventeen and excelled in several ways. He completed two world tours during peacetime. During these tours, he became first mate and manned the main gun on the ship. Upon leaving the Navy, he played semi-professional minor league baseball in Virginia, then known as the Clover League and today known as the Appalachian League, and was paid a monthly salary to travel with the team. After he left baseball, he had a few different jobs and then made a career out of driving a semi-truck across the country. He was definitely a traveler, to say the least.

Fast forward many years, and there he was, driving a big rig along Interstate 40 in middle Tennessee, just a few miles outside the mountaintop community of Monterey, my mother's hometown. A very dangerous winter storm was moving through the area, and travel was extremely treacherous. Much to his surprise, Bill spotted a young girl walking down the side of the interstate, trudging through the new-fallen snow.

There are so many ways that this story could have ended tragically. He could have been a serial killer. *She* could have been a serial killer. The truck could have crashed and gone over the side of the mountain. One or both of them could have ended up in deep trouble with the law, her for being a teenager runaway or him taking an underage girl out of state. As it turned out, none of those things happened. Instead, eventually, I happened.

I should mention that, in the beginning, Daddy didn't know that Mom was not of legal age (understandably, she certainly didn't volunteer that piece of information, given her rather desperate situation). Thinking that she was just another hitchhiker, Bill allowed Becky to climb up into his truck, and then he continued on his run. At that time (back in the early 1980s), hitchhiking was fairly common (although perhaps less so during a major snowstorm), and it was not unusual for truckers to pick up people who needed a ride to the next town or even to the other coast. Becky began traveling with Bill all over the United States, and I'm sure you can figure out the rest of the story because here I am all these years later, the daughter of Becky Allen and Bill Simmons.

My dad was originally from Virginia but had some family in the Coalmont/Altamont area of Tennessee. So, when it came close to the time for Momma to give birth to me, they stayed in that area with some of Daddy's family, and that is where I was born, in a little country doctor's office in a small-town in Grundy County, Tennessee, called Altamont. This doctor's office was called the Cathedral Canyon Clinic and was run solely by Dr. Harbolt and his wife. My dad later told me that Dr. Harbolt only charged them $6 for office visits and $150 to deliver me when the time came.

The clinic was very simple and old-fashioned. They didn't do a lot of things they do in hospitals now like epidurals. My mom was in labor with me for thirty-six hours with no epidural, completely natural childbirth. She had to be thinking, Boy, if we ain't off to a good start with this one! And she was right. This was just a small clue as to what was to follow, which was a lot of heartache, pain, and suffering. Of course, it wasn't all bad. There were good times, but sadly, most of what I remember about that time of my life is very painful. Even all this time later, it is very difficult for me to think about, much less talk about or write about my early childhood years. Still, the story must be told if you are to fully understand all that I went through in order to find myself in that cow pasture on that cold October night, finally crying out to God. So, here goes.

Everything was kind of normal for a while. My mom, Becky, stayed with some of my dad's family in the Altamont area after I was born. My dad, Bill, drove an 18-wheeler and was on the road most of the time. I was my mom's first and only child. My dad had other children from a previous relationship, but they lived in another state with their mother. I did not meet them until I was much older.

When I was still very small, we moved to McMinnville, Tennessee, and we lived in an area known as Smartt Station. We had a really nice home in a great neighborhood, and, for a while, things were good. Our house wasn't very big, but it was plenty big enough for us. It was a nice, cozy, little, blue house with a huge yard where I had plenty of room to run and play. I had my own little playhouse and a swing set outback. I really thought I was something special back then, and I guess I was to my parents.

My mom and I faithfully attended a local church right down the road from our house. I absolutely loved church and rarely missed it. I received award pins for six weeks, six months, and one year of perfect attendance in Sunday school. My mom stayed at home with me while my Dad worked. She seemed like the perfect stay-at-home mom in those early years. She took care of me while my dad was gone and took care of him when he was home. Her life revolved around her family. She not only took care of me and my dad but also all of my animals.

I became an animal lover at a very early age. I absolutely loved my cats and dogs and other critters! I had a small black poodle named Fi-Fi that my parents got for me when she was just a tiny puppy, and I was just around two years old. I also had a white cat named Sugar and a calico one named Spice. From the outside looking in, it looked like we had the perfect little family—Sugar, Spice, and everything nice, as the saying goes. However, if you had walked through the door and stayed awhile, you would have left thinking quite differently. It wasn't a very good place to live when my dad was home because my parents didn't get along very well. It was really hard on me emotionally because I was a daddy's girl, and I wanted my daddy home. When he was home, though, it seemed like all they did was fight.

My worst memory of them fighting was when I was around four or five years old. Neither of them hurt the other physically, but there was a lot of screaming and commotion going on. My dad was drinking like he usually did every weekend when he was home. Daddy and Momma were fighting, as usual, but this time Momma decided to leave, and she was intent on taking me with her. My dad wasn't having it. He didn't want us to go.

My mom had me wrapped in my favorite patchwork quilt that she had made for me. I loved it. It was so soft. The squares had blue, pink, and white in them, with little pink yarn coming through the top of each square. The memory of the quilt is probably so vivid to me now because that quilt was the only piece of comfort I had at the time. The quilt had become my covering and my protector because those who were supposed to be taking care of me were on the verge of separating, and, deep down, I knew it. I was scared. I didn't want to leave my daddy, but I didn't want to stay with him when he was like that either. He wasn't mean to me or anything when he drank. He actually *never ever* laid a hand on me, not to even spank me when I was growing up, but I still didn't like to be around him when he was drinking. The fighting between him and Momma scared me.

had me wrapped in my blanket and was holding me. We were standing at the front door, in the entryway of our home. Daddy begged her not to leave. I was so upset and confused. I didn't understand what was going on. I didn't want to leave my daddy, but I didn't want to stay like this either. I didn't really have a choice in the matter, of course. Momma had me in her arms. Daddy was holding the front door closed, but somehow Momma got past him and through the door. We left.

My parents had begun having marital problems way before this incident when I was very young. It had been going on for as long as I could remember. They really loved one another, but both had a lot of baggage from their past, and neither of them knew how to deal with it or give it to the Lord. I don't think they knew how to let go of all the hurt and pain, so they carried the scars and burdens of their childhoods over into every relationship they entered. It was then compiled and carried over into their marriage. This is all too common in our world and represents a vicious cycle caused by our enemy, the devil; he destroys as many people, marriages, and families as he can. He is the father of lies.

Looking back at my parents' separation and eventual divorce, I cannot imagine how hard it was on each of them because I know they really loved each other. They always did, even years after they split up. Daddy offered to come home more than once, and Momma told me that my dad was the only man that she ever really loved. They just couldn't get along. They didn't know how because no one had ever taught them how to function in a mature relationship. Tragically, all they knew to do was to fight, and that didn't help anything at all. It just made things worse.

As for me, personally, the breakup of my parents' marriage was just one of many attempts by the enemy to destroy my life, maybe even to *end* my life, from a very early age. When I was less than two years old, I got pneumonia and almost died because I was severely dehydrated. The nurses tried to get an IV into my arm, but they couldn't because my veins kept "rolling," which means that every time they tried to get the needle in the vein, it would move. Momma said it was so bad she was afraid she was going to lose me.

Then, a few months later, my mom and I were in a car accident in my mom's hometown. We had gone to visit Nanny, my mom's mom, when a drunk driver hit us. The impact was so severe that our car flipped over several times and ended up in someone's yard. My mom was pinned inside in the vehicle and worried that it might blow up, so she unsnapped my car seat and had me crawl out. When help arrived, they got Momma out of the car. She didn't have any bad injuries. I had the worst of it, but nothing was life-threatening. My left arm was broken, and I had a gash below my right eye. It was a miracle that, at just two years old, I was able to crawl out of the car with a broken arm and only needed a cast and a few stitches. There was a lot of foreshadowing in that event; there would be many times in my life when I found myself in situations that looked impossible to overcome, but yet I did.

At about age three, I started having stomach problems. Over time, the stomach problems became more severe, to the point where I vomited blood. My parents were worried that something was seriously wrong with me. They took me to the doctor, but there was never a definite diagnosis. Momma told me later she thought I had a "nervous" stomach. I believe my stomach problems were caused by the stress of my parents' marital problems because my health issues got much better for a period of time after my parents separated.

The dysfunction of my parents' marriage affected me both physically and psychologically. Not only did I endure the pain and discomfort of my "nervous" stomach, but I also developed emotional problems too. It started with me throwing awful temper tantrums when I was very small. Honestly, I was just repeating the behavior I was seeing: fussing, fighting, and throwing fits. My parents would not only verbally argue, but they would physically fight as well. I don't remember my dad ever hurting or injuring my mom. From what I remember and what I have been told, from his side was mostly verbal attacks, but from her side, it was mostly physical abuse against him. Since that's what I saw my parents do, that's what I did.

My mom and dad probably tried to teach me the right way by what they were telling me to do, but they were not *showing* me the right way by their actions. That old saying, "Do as I say, not as I do," doesn't work. How we act in front of our children carries much more weight than what we say in front of them. Now that I am a parent myself, I realize that, although it does matter what we say, our behavior is much more important because that is what our children are much more likely to model and imitate.

Later, when I was about five, I had a little glass monkey that was inside a "jail cell." One day, I threw the glass monkey, and I broke it. I became hysterical because I had broken my treasured toy. I can still remember the frustration and sense of loss. It was a brown, glass monkey in a small metal jail cell with a little metal lock and keys. I loved it because I could open up the cell, get the monkey out, and then lock it back up. It is so telling now to see how my first memory of a temper tantrum had to do with a monkey in a jail cell. It's like it was a picture of me. I was already becoming bound by anger and rage at the tender age of five. Sadly, that toy was just the first of many "monkeys" that would be on my back over the next two decades. It would take my total surrender to the Lord to overcome the many emotional problems that I can now trace back to my early childhood and the extremely dysfunctional family in which I grew up (not to mention the ongoing effects of the terrible situations in which my parents themselves were raised). Praise be to Him; however, in time, I was to overcome all of that early trauma when I finally dedicated my life to Christ. Unfortunately, there would be nearly twenty years of heartache before that happened.

Chapter Three

The Effects of Divorce

I was six years old when my mom officially filed for divorce. It wasn't a messy divorce. There were no big court battles over who got what, who would have custody, or how much child support would be paid. My mom had never worked during their marriage, so my dad gave her the home, the car, alimony, and child support. She was also given full custody of me; he didn't put up any fight on the matter because he was on the road working the majority of the time.

My dad got the usual weekend and holiday visitation. That's really all we saw each other anyway, even when my parents were married. Now that I am grown, I realize that this was due to the fact that he had to make a living and support his family, but as a child, I didn't understand. All I knew was I wanted to spend more time with my daddy, and I didn't get to.

Momma and Daddy got along for the most part once they were no longer living together. Their parting seemed peaceful enough, but everyone knows that there is really nothing peaceful about divorce, especially when children are involved. My first-grade teacher let me bring my favorite baby doll, a Cabbage Patch Premie with a yellow and white outfit, to school during the divorce because I was having such a hard time with the separation. I felt like my whole world was being torn apart. Even though my parents fought, part of me still wanted them to be together. I was just a little kid who wanted both my mommy and my daddy to live with me in our house, and I didn't understand why that couldn't happen anymore. It was a very frightening and confusing time in my life. I simply could not understand all the things that were happening, especially why my daddy couldn't live with me anymore. I felt like he was leaving me, like there was something wrong with me, like he didn't want me anymore, and like he didn't love me after the separation.

There are certain times and situations that stick out in my mind about that time period, like the details of my baby doll I held onto during the divorce and during specific times when my parents argued. For some reason, I always seem to remember the hard times instead of the good times. I'm not sure why. Maybe it's because it was traumatic to me, and it caused those memories to be etched in my mind. I know there were good times. I have a few pictures in which we are all smiling and getting along, but, for some reason, I can't remember very much about the happier days. I just remember being upset when my parents were together and fought so much and then being broken-hearted when they decided they should go their separate ways. Maybe it seems contradictory, but it really wasn't. I wanted them to stay together, stop fighting, and be happy, just as any child would have wanted. Every child wants that, but it seems that fewer and fewer actually get it. We live in a very fallen world, and the "sins of the father" (and mother) bring many unfortunate consequences on the children.

After the divorce was finalized, Daddy came and got me every weekend there for a while. We would usually go shopping and out to eat. Not too long after the divorce, however, my dad moved in with another woman, Gail, my soon-to-be stepmother. They lived in Nashville, a couple of hours away from where Momma and I were staying at that time. I visited with them a few weekends at their apartment, but that didn't last long.

The visits between my father and me grew fewer and farther between. Eventually, it got to the point that I very rarely saw my daddy. It was very hurtful and confusing. I didn't understand why he didn't come get me anymore. I didn't understand what had changed. I knew he had a new girlfriend, but I still didn't understand why he couldn't (or wouldn't) come get me when he was supposed to. I knew he had loved me and my mom at one time, but I was starting to question if that was still the case.

Back when he was still picking me up every weekend, there was one particular day he had taken me to our favorite restaurant, Bonanza. It was just me and him. I was sitting there across the table from him, enjoying a nice hot bowl of my favorite soup, when Daddy started crying. I don't remember ever seeing my daddy cry before that moment, and it wasn't just a few tears. It was real, flowing tears; he was sobbing. I went over to comfort him and tell him I was sorry and ask him if he was okay. Remember, I was just six years old, so I didn't understand that my dad was more than likely crying because he was hurt and remorseful over the divorce and the way things had turned out. I don't think he ever wanted the divorce or ever wanted to leave us. Now, looking back, I don't think he could emotionally handle being around us much after that. So, that's when he did what he did best back then, and that was to run. That was the last time I remember him coming to pick me up and take me out by himself. After that weekend, he started to move on with his life—and his new girlfriend.

After the visits had almost stopped, there was one weekend that Daddy was supposed to come and get me. One of my friends was having a birthday party, but I wouldn't go because I wanted to see my daddy. I wasn't about to risk not getting to see my daddy just for some cake and ice cream! If there was even the slightest chance that I would get to see him, I wasn't budging. Momma kept trying to talk me into going to the party. I guess she figured he wasn't coming, and I'm sure that it was hard on her to see me hurt like that and to watch me sit for hours waiting for my daddy to show up. Even with her pleading, I still wouldn't go. Instead, I sat there on our front porch all day, just waiting for my daddy to come get me, and he never showed up.

I was crushed. Even though I was still just a little girl, I began to feel abandoned and rejected by the man that I had loved more than any other man in the world. The man I thought would be there for the rest of my life, at least the rest of his life, the man I thought was supposed to take care of me and love me and protect me, was, for all intents and purposes, gone from my life. I didn't know why he wasn't there or why he didn't love me enough to at least come and see me on the weekends like he used to. In many ways, it felt like he had left me, not my mom.

So, there I was, at six years old, feeling abandoned, rejected, broken, and confused. I didn't understand how my once loving father had moved on so quickly and how he could have a whole new family without me. It didn't seem like long at all before he had a new wife, a new family, and a new life, and I didn't even get to be a part of it. I had accepted that my parents couldn't get along and that my father had moved on. While I didn't like that my parents had divorced, on some level, I understood that it was best for them (but not for me). Although I actually liked my stepmother and enjoyed the little time we were able to spend together, I didn't get the opportunity to be a part of their new family in any significant way.

After a while, I didn't even see my father on my birthday or holidays anymore. We did talk on the phone every once in a while, if something was wrong or if I needed something. My stepmother sent child support payments and gifts by mail for my birthday and holidays. If Daddy had a truck run close to where I lived, he would sometimes stop by to see me for a few minutes and give me some money, but he was never able to stay long because of his work schedule. I didn't understand why I couldn't be a part of his life anymore. Momma tried to tell me that my daddy loved me, I had a good daddy, and he loved me the best he could due to the situation, but I couldn't see that at the time.

As scarce as our time together became, honestly, there were times I thought it would have been easier if I didn't see him at all because it was so hard on me afterward when I did get to visit with him. Deep down, though, I still needed my father in my life and wanted to spend time with him. It seemed that the more I longed for a connection with him during that time, the more distant that connection became. It was extremely painful for me and left a wound deep within my heart.

Eventually, as I got older, I basically stopped even attempting to have a relationship with my dad because I had felt so rejected for so long. I couldn't take a chance on being rejected all over again. Just seeing him would bring up all the same old questions. *Why? Why don't you love me? Why don't you want me? Why don't you want to spend time with me?* These questions, along with other circumstances, eventually led me into all kinds of very unhealthy and dysfunctional relationships.

Although it felt so very personal to me at the time, I now realize that I was just one of the thousands of children who went through the trauma of their parents' divorce and, in many cases, estrangement from one or both parents during the 1980s and 1990s, when the divorce rate was skyrocketing across this country.

Divorce is never an easy thing. It can be downright heart-wrenching, and everyone involved in a divorce gets hurt, but this is especially true for the children. As a child, many times, you start to question and wonder if it was somehow your fault. Maybe you weren't good enough, maybe you did something wrong, or maybe your mom or dad didn't love you enough. I believe this is one way the devil uses divorce to begin tearing children down at an early age. The devil wants you, the child, to feel rejected by the one person who was supposed to love you and protect you, which leaves you feeling unloved, unwanted, and inadequate.

This can lead to all sorts of trouble later in life, such as inferiority complexes, low self-esteem, poor self-image, and searching for love in all the wrong places. This is exactly what happened to me. I ended up having so many issues in my teenage years and into my twenties, most of which were rooted in the feeling that my daddy did not want me or love me enough to stay in my life. Because I lacked a healthy relationship with my father and had begun to believe the devil's lies about the reasons for that, I felt unloved, unwanted, and inadequate. I suffered from low self-esteem and a poor self-image, and I definitely looked for love in all the wrong places.

It's taken me years of heartache and tears to learn the truth, and the truth is that, in reality, divorce very rarely has anything to do with the children. The problem truly lies between the mother and the father. However, the devil uses divorce to create strongholds and wrong mindsets by making you think your mother or father left you, the child. It is just one of the so many lies that the enemy tries to feed us. For the devil "is a liar, and the father of it" (John 8:44).

The truth is that if your parents are divorced, your parent left his or her spouse, your mother or father, not you. It was their problem, not yours, that led to the break-up. If your relationship with your non-custodial parent didn't survive your parents' divorce, this is not your fault. Let's say that again: it is *not your fault*. You were a child. They were adults.

Still, children of divorce often grow up believing the lies. This, in turn, can result in the child growing up to be a very different, highly damaged version of who God created him or her to be. At the very least, this can cause rejection, abandonment, and trust issues. Again, this is exactly what happened to me (and much, much more).

Divorce can also create one of two fears in children whose parents have chosen to part ways. The first is the fear of letting anyone get too close because that person may leave you or hurt you like your parent did. In this case, you keep everyone at a distance and won't let them in close enough to hurt you. The other extreme is the fear of rejection, being alone, and not being loved. In this case, you cling to and hang on to everyone you care about no matter what kind of negative consequence the relationship may have on you and your well-being. This can include the development of codependent behavior, also known as relationship addiction. Some people may even bounce back and forth between these two extremes, being too clingy one minute and then pushing others away the next. This was the case for me for many years.

Because of what happened with my parents' marriage and the resulting estrangement between my father and me, I ended up in all kinds of unhealthy relationships. It seemed like I let the wrong ones in and pushed the right ones out. Somehow, I could deal better with the more abusive friends and significant others who came into my life than I could deal with just "regular" people. It became normal to me; as dysfunctional as it was, it was what I was used to by that time. Maybe it was just what I felt that I deserved. As bizarre as it sounds now, the more someone mistreated me, the clingier I became; maybe their behavior felt "right" because it was so very familiar to me. Those who were "normal," so to speak, I ran from. I put walls up and pushed them out. Part of me knew I was anything but normal, and I had no idea how to have healthy relationships with normal people.

Chapter Four

Me and Momma

After the divorce, Momma completed her GED (general education diploma) so that she could enroll in college. Because she had dropped out of high school midway through her senior year, so she did not have a regular diploma. While she was still receiving regular alimony and child support payments from my dad, she took a few classes, but when the alimony payments stopped (they were only temporary and had a defined stopping point), Momma had to quit taking classes and start working in order to make ends meet. Unfortunately, her income from working did not completely replace the money lost from the alimony payments, and, as a result, we lost my childhood home during that time and had to move into an apartment.

This event was the catalyst for the drifting lifestyle that would plague our lives for many years to come. It was hard growing up like that, wandering from place to place without any real sense of having a home of our own. I never felt settled. Every time that it felt like we might finally be putting down some roots, something else would come up, and we would be on the move again. The lack of stability and general financial distress of those years took a heavy toll on both me and my mother.

In my third-grade year, Momma and I moved to Huntsville, Alabama. She had gotten a job as a greeter at the Huntsville Space and Rocket Center. I thought she had the most awesome job in the world. In reality, it was just an entry-level position and paid very little, but to me, it was fascinating. We both adjusted well to our new surroundings, quickly making new friends and starting a new life.

Of course, right when it felt like everything was starting to look up, the bottom fell out. My dad skipped town. He left my stepmom, Gail, and no one knew where he was. My stepmother had been the one who made out the child support checks. She wasn't getting Daddy's paychecks, so we didn't get any child support. Momma didn't make enough money on her own to support us in Huntsville, so we had to move back to McMinnville, Tennessee. We stayed with some of Momma's friends there until she could get back on her feet.

I remember being very fearful and anxious during that time. The sensation of having the rug jerked out from under us just as we were starting to stand on our own was very disorienting. Most of all, I felt a huge sense of disappointment at the prospect of having to start over yet again. The image I had of my family back in our little blue house in McMinnville grew further and further away in my mind. Instead of Momma and me moving towards some sense of happiness or at least stability, our lives were going the opposite direction—a direction that was scary to me, even as a child. I had no home to speak of, and I didn't know what was going to happen to me or my mother. I also didn't know what had become of my father. Was he okay? Was he safe? Had something happened to him? I'm still not sure what happened between him and my stepmom back then. I only know that his leaving like that greatly affected me.

After some time, my father turned up again, got back together with my stepmother, and moved with her to Bristol, Virginia. The bad news was that Bristol was even farther away from Momma and me than Nashville had been. The good news was that my stepmom started sending child support payments again. Momma got a job, and we were able to move into a small one-bedroom apartment of our own in McMinnville. It wasn't much, but it was livable.

As it turned out, we didn't get to stay there very long before we had a full-time, live-in guest. My grandmother, Nanny, was hurt on the job in the nursing home where she worked, and she had to have surgery. By this time, Momma and Nanny's relationship, while far from perfect, had at least stabilized to the point that Momma felt that it was her place to take care of Nanny after her surgery. In some ways, having my grandmother there with us was comforting because, despite her many faults, I knew that she loved me. On the other hand, Nanny was still Nanny, and there was always a certain undercurrent of animosity between her and Momma. When Nanny healed from the surgery, she moved back to her house in Monterey but was never able to go back to work again. Instead, she began drawing Social Security Disability payments.

Soon after Nanny went home, Momma and I moved again. By this time, I was in the fourth grade. Our new apartment was somewhat of an upgrade. It was a little nicer, and it had two bedrooms instead of just one. It felt really good to finally have my own room again. Momma had a job at a junkyard. The job paid decently, but, in the end, the money wasn't worth what we went through during that time. Momma met a man at work, Don. She fell head over heels for him, and things began to change really fast. I'd like to say that our situation improved, but that would be far from the truth. In fact, things took a huge turn for the worse. Momma had already been dating a little here and there and had started drinking a little. When she fell for Don, however, the drinking and clubbing went to a whole new level. They would go to the local VFW Club (technically a private club for veterans of foreign wars but in reality just another local bar) and drink almost every weekend, leaving me at home or with neighbors to fend for myself for hours on end. When they weren't out in a bar or club, Don was at our house a lot, and he would often be drunk while he was there. Momma really didn't drink a whole lot at home at that point, which was the one good thing. Eventually, Momma found out that Don was married, but she had already fallen hard for him and wouldn't let him go. He promised her that he would leave his wife. He eventually did, but never filed for divorce.

They started fighting a lot. Don would get mean and push Momma around when he was drinking. It was very scary to me when that happened. My mom and dad had fought, but they never really hurt each other bad physically. Most of their fighting had been verbal. Don was the opposite of my daddy in that respect; Don had no problem putting his hands on my momma and hurting her. If anything, he seemed to enjoy exerting his physical advantage over her. He was quite a large guy, not just heavy but talk ad stocky as well.

One night, things got so bad that I had to run out of our apartment to call the police. The apartments we lived in at the time were two stories, and we lived on the second floor. The stairs leading from the first floor to the second floor were outside, and they were concrete. This particular night when Momma and Don were fighting, she tried to run away to call the police, but he ran down the stairs after her and dragged her by the hair of her head back up the stairs. I was scared to death. Even though Don had never hurt me, I was terrified of what he might do to my momma. I ran past them down the stairs to the neighbor's apartment and called the police. I stayed at the neighbor's apartment until the officers came. When he realized that the cops had been called, Don got scared and left. Despite him hurting her over and over again, Momma refused to file criminal charges against him.

Meanwhile, Nanny's health continued to deteriorate. So, in my fifth-grade year, we moved to Monterey, my mom's hometown, to be closer to Nanny and help her. We rented a really nice, two-bedroom townhouse right in the middle of town. Don moved there with us. In spite of what he had done to my mom, I liked him on some level. I don't know if the trauma in my life had become so familiar that it didn't occur to me to not like him or whether it was just that even a poor excuse for a pseudo-stepfather was better than no father figure at all. As I said, he never hit me, and he was, at the very least, a modest source of financial stability. I believe Momma thought that by taking him to Monterey, it would somehow alleviate the problems they had in McMinnville. Either that or she just simply couldn't let him go.

After we moved to Monterey, Momma went to the local church where she had been baptized as a teenager to inquire about attending church there again. She spoke with the pastor. She was honest and told him she was living with a married man. The pastor told her she wasn't welcome in their church. At the time, I didn't really understand much about church or the Bible, but now that I do, I have some really serious issues with the way this was handled and how my mom was treated. If things had been handled differently and Momma had been accepted rather than rejected by this pastor, our lives could have possibly been so massively different. Maybe she would have eventually been able to get free from the life she was living and the road she was beginning to go down, which would have significantly changed the course of not only her life but mine as well. Instead, we continued down a slippery slope that eventually landed me in the cow pasture hiding from the law under a pile of logs on that October night in 2004.

• • •

Yes, my mom was going down the wrong road and was living wrong, but she was still very young, not even thirty years old at this time, and she had not had a very good raising or a proper example set before her growing up. The job of the church is to take in those who are hurting and/or struggling and love them and show them the way to live, not to turn them away and leave them to their own devices and the ways of the world. My mother was indeed a sinner, and she needed God in the worst way at that time in her life.

The fact that her previous home church turned my momma away in her time of need still makes me angry, to be quite honest. I have forgiven and even understand the situation. However, as you will see, it wasn't very long after this happened that our lives took a very sharp turn for the worse. My mom was reaching out for help because she knew that what she was doing was wrong. That's why she confessed her sins to the pastor and told him she wanted to get back into church. If you read the Bible, you know that, although Jesus did tell people to go and sin no more, He never condemned them for their wrongdoing—not even the woman who was caught in the very act of adultery (see John 8).

I have heard the word "Christian" defined as "a little of Christ." I don't believe the way the pastor treated my mom was very Christ-like, and neither did she. She told him that a church should be a hospital for sinners, not a sanctuary for saints. I agree. We are supposed to love people like Jesus did. We are not to condone their sin, but we are supposed to love them, even in the midst of their sin. Individuals living in active sin (adultery, addiction, abuse, etc.) do not need to be in leadership positions in the church, but they do need to be *in church*. Jesus Himself said, "Those who are well have no need of a physician, but those who are sick [do]" and "I did not come to call the righteous, but sinners to repentance" (Matthew 9:12, 13). Jesus does not expect us to save ourselves. If this was possible, there would have been no need for Him to sacrifice His life for ours on the cross.

I believe lots of people, both in the church and the unchurched, get it mixed up. They think the sinner has to get things right and *then* go to God, but it just does not work that way. If we could fix ourselves, we wouldn't need God. The fact is, we can't change on our own. We need Christ's life-transforming power in order to accomplish this. He takes us as we are and gradually makes us into who He would have us to be. We are transformed into His image from glory to glory (2 Corinthians 3:18). Christ accepts us as we are, but He loves us too much to leave us that way!

● ● ●

Despite what happened with Momma and the church, we adjusted to being back in her hometown. Monterey is an extremely small town, the kind of place where everybody knows everybody, which can be both positive and negative. Momma became reacquainted with old friends, and I made some new ones. One of my new friends was a girl named Nadine, who lived across the street from us. The other was Lori, whom I still consider to be my best friend today.

Nadine, her mother, and her little sister attended a local church. I went with them most of the time. My mom went a few times, but not on a regular basis. She never was able to fully get back into church regularly after what happened to her with that particular pastor when we first moved back to Monterey.

In sixth grade, I made the cheerleading squad, which helped me to fit in at school and make even more friends. Momma had been a cheerleader when she was in high school, so she held cheerleading practices for us in our backyard after school. We'd have drinks and snacks and do fun, normal kid stuff. I was finally starting to have a somewhat normal childhood again, complete with good friends and good times. I also had the benefit of having some extended family living in the area, including my aunt and uncle, my great-grandparents, and some cousins.

That relatively pleasant and stable phase of my life would soon end, however, and we would be wandering again. Interestingly enough, I don't recall what happened between Momma and Don. All I remember is that, after they split up and he moved out, we had to move out of our apartment and into Nanny's house. Yes, *Nanny's house* (that alone should tell you how desperate our situation had become). Without Don's income, Momma couldn't afford to keep our place any longer. Things would only go further downhill from there.

Chapter Five

My Dysfunctional Family Tree

When my mom and I moved in with Nanny in the fall of 1992, it was just me, Momma, and Nanny. My aunt and uncle were living on their own at the time. My Uncle Nick, my mom's brother, was living with his girlfriend in Clarkrange, a very small rural town about twenty minutes away from Monterey. Clarkrange had been known as "Crankrange" for years because of all the crank in the area. In case you don't already know, crank is a form of methamphetamine similar to crystal meth. It's a type of "speed," a powerful stimulant that can, at a minimum, disrupt the user's sleep cycle and, when taken in heavier amounts, can cause the user to become extremely paranoid and even hallucinate.

My uncle had used drugs and alcohol for as long as I could remember. He started using when he was a teenager. I really didn't understand much about drugs myself at the time we moved in with Nanny. I was only ten years old, and all I knew about drugs was what I had learned in DARE, the Drug Awareness Resistance Education program at school, where they told us how bad drugs were, how they would harm your body, and how they would get you in trouble. I was about to get an up-close and personal crash course on the reality of what drugs can do to someone.

Early one morning, when I was getting ready to go to school, Uncle Nick unexpectedly showed up at Nanny's house. He was completely out of his mind on crank and cocaine, high on not just one, but two, different types of speed. A friend of his told us that Uncle Nick had done an "eight ball" (the slang term for 3.5 grams—1/8 of an ounce) of each all at once by himself. From what I now understand, that's more than enough speed to kill someone. I'm not sure how long Uncle Nick had gone without sleep, but by the time he came to my Nanny's, he was hallucinating and in really bad shape.

I was just a little kid needing to get ready for school, but Uncle Nick was very paranoid because of the drugs pulsing through his system. Therefore, he wouldn't let us do certain things. Because he thought that there were cops everywhere and that they were watching us, he wouldn't let us talk out loud. Instead, we had to whisper. He wouldn't let us turn on the television because he said that he needed to be listening to the police (or whatever he thought he was hearing). He wouldn't let us walk around the house like normal people. We had to duck down anytime we walked in front of the windows. To explain a bit further, my uncle didn't just think that a couple of local Monterey police officers were cruising by Nanny's house in search of him; he thought there were all kinds of cops, FBI (Federal Bureau of Investigation), TBI (Tennessee Bureau of Investigation), CIA (Central Intelligence Agency), DEA (Drug Enforcement Agency), you name it. In his mind, he was convinced that there were dozens of law enforcement officers sitting in vans surrounding Nanny's house, hiding up the trees, and crouched in the bushes and that they were all there to take him to jail.

Of course, in reality, there wasn't anybody outside except maybe a neighbor or two walking their dog or taking their trash out, but there was no telling Uncle Nick that. As I would find out during my own years of involvement in the drug culture, when you're on that kind of speed and haven't had enough sleep, you begin to hear and see all kinds of things that are not real. To the person who is hallucinating, what they hear and see is as real to them as reading this book is to you. It is especially common for heavy users of methamphetamines like crystal meth and crank to "geek" or "tweak" about the police, meaning they have paranoid delusions and hallucinations. It all comes from (a very understandable) fear of being busted. Living on the edge of the law, sometimes for years on end, causes the user to become extremely paranoid and to "see" law enforcement officers all around them like Uncle Nick did that morning. Of course, it is possible that the police may, in fact, be watching when someone is involved in that kind of activity (especially if they are a dealer or trafficker), but very rarely to the extent the paranoid person believes.

Momma knew I had to go to school, and Nanny's nerves were all to pieces. So, Momma went riding around with my uncle so that Nanny could have some peace and I could get to school. It's still kind of hard for me to think of my Uncle Nick in that kind of shape. He was always an easy-going, laid-back kind of guy. He loved me and was great with me; it had always been that way, ever since I was very little. I loved him so much. He was an amazing person when he was sober or even somewhat sober. Of course, I had seen him use illegal substances before. I knew he and some of his friends passed a "cigarette" around in the back room in my presence when I was younger. I had pretty much figured out they were smoking a joint and not a real cigarette, but marijuana never made Uncle Nick act like this. I had seen him come to Nanny's intoxicated to the point where she had to lock him out of the house once because he had become a mean drunk, but that only happened one time that I can remember (when I was about six years old).

This person who was in front of me now (I was ten years old, and he was around twenty-two) was not the Uncle Nick I knew and loved. This guy had lost his mind, and I didn't know where my real Uncle Nick was. I just wanted him back because this guy scared me. He did not do anything abusive or threatening toward us, but his mental state was freaking me out. It made me wonder if there really were all these people outside or if he was crazy. I wondered if he would ever be okay again. I didn't really understand that he was high on speed and that it was the effects of the drugs that were making him flip out. My mom tried to explain it to me later, but, as the events were happening that morning, I didn't understand. Honestly, even after she explained it, I still didn't fully understand. What ten-year-old would be able to truly comprehend something like that?

Momma told me later that, when she and Uncle Nick were out driving around so that Nanny and I could be spared the worst of this breakdown, they passed several people that they knew. Although some of these individuals were longtime friends of the family, Uncle Nick believed that they were undercover cops and driving in unmarked vehicles. Momma tried to talk him into going to the hospital, rehab, or somewhere to get some help, but he wouldn't go—not even for her.

Finally, he let her call a sheriff's deputy, a man who had known our family for years. The officer agreed not to arrest Uncle Nick if he would go to a hospital and get help. Consequently, my uncle was taken to Moccasin Bend Mental Health Institute, about one hundred miles or so away in Chattanooga, Tennessee. Once he was admitted and had begun detoxification to get the drugs out of his system, he still stayed up for eight days. Eight days! That, or course, was in addition to however long he had already been up when he arrived on Nanny's doorstep that morning. After he finally came down and got some sleep, the hospital released him and let him come home. Sadly, his drug and alcohol problem did not end there. In fact, that whole terrifying episode didn't even slow him down. Things continued to get worse for him, much worse, in fact. Uncle Nick's problems with drugs and alcohol would eventually result in him being arrested multiple times and in him serving time in jail after a drug conviction (more on that later).

Looking back, it's obvious that we were a very dysfunctional family. At the time, however, I did not understand life in those terms. We were, in my mind, a close-knit family. It was very frightening to ten-year-old me to watch someone I loved spiral out of control like that. The trauma of that day has left the incident very vivid in my mind, even though many years have passed since that crazy morning when all I wanted to do was get to school on time. I can remember being so afraid that Uncle Nick would never be the same again. Those fears were not totally unfounded. He did change in several respects as a result of that episode, and he was never quite the same again. I don't remember him ever fully becoming his loving, carefree self after that terrible day.

This seems like a good time to tell you a little more history from my mother's side of the family. I will need to go back a few generations so that you can better understand the family dynamics and the many layers of dysfunction that not only formed the backdrop for my uncle's drug-fueled paranoia but also helped pave the road that led to my night in the cow pasture in 2004.

Momma's family history is especially important because I grew up knowing my mother's people much better than I knew my father's family. Most of the information I am going to share at this time is not firsthand knowledge but was given to me over the years by my mother and others outside of our family. My great-grandfather, Amos Allen, is as good a place to start as any. I called him "Grandpa Amos," even though he was actually my mother's grandpa, not mine; as I explained earlier, my own maternal grandfather died (in a supposed "jailhouse suicide" after having been convicted of murder) in 1971, a decade before I was born. Like his father before him, Grandpa Amos had a drinking problem when he was a young man. He was one of the youngest children in his father's second family. Because his own father died when he was just five years old, Grandpa Amos didn't have that strong paternal presence that boys need during his formative years. As a result, it took him a very long time to learn how to be a good man.

    He and my great-grandmother, Harriet, who I called "Granny Harriet," married in 1925 when Grandpa Amos was twenty, and she was just sixteen. Harriet's own father was still living at the time, but he was prone to going off and staying gone for long periods of time and was never one to be accused of hard work. Although it may have seemed like she was improving her lot in life by getting married and moving away from the poverty that had befallen her mother and siblings after her father's desertion, she actually just traded one version of a hard life for another. Grandpa Amos's heavy drinking, and the physical violence that often accompanied it, took its toll on the young couple. They had a very troublesome marriage, marrying one another not only once but twice. According to the family, they almost married a third time, but instead, Grandpa Amos married another woman. Many years later, Grandpa Amos and his second wife gave their lives to the Lord and joined a local church, where they were active until he passed away in his mid-eighties.

My Granny Harriet, on the other hand, was a completely different story. She never remarried and spent the rest of her life alone. She never went to church or gave her heart to the Lord, as far as I know. She never even went to her sons' funerals when they each died. Amos and Harriet had five children together—four boys and one girl. One of those boys was my grandfather, Oden Allen; all four boys died fairly young and tragically. Granny Harriet was a very "different" type of person, to say the least. I loved her, but she and the way she lived out in the woods with very few neighbors scared me as a little child.

Some people around Monterey even said that Granny Harriet was a witch because she was a fortune-teller who read palms and tarot cards (I have since been told that her own mother did those things, too). I never bought into that "she-is-a-witch" stuff when I was growing up, mainly because Granny Harriet and Momma were very close, and I just didn't think of Granny Harriet in those terms. Instead, I chose to disregard what I had been told by others around town. Now that I am older and understand the Bible, however, I must admit that she would have been considered a witch and that what she did would have been considered witchcraft. It really makes me wonder if all that she went through—losing her sons, dying alone, the generational curses that went down the line from that point on—were in connection to her (and perhaps her mother's) participation in witchcraft.

I really don't know if she even understood enough of the teachings of the Bible to know that what she was doing was wrong or if she had any idea the effect that her actions were having upon her or her family. As I said, both she and Grandpa Amos had it rough growing up, both coming from families that were far from ideal. Maybe the generational curses started even before Granny Harriet; it's hard to say, not knowing all that came earlier in the history of their families. Either way, there definitely seemed to be some type of darkness that permeated over her and over the next generations, including my grandpa Oden and his brothers, my mother and her siblings and cousins, and me.

I never met my maternal grandfather, Oden, the one I mentioned earlier in the book, who died while incarcerated when Momma was only nine years old. I'm going to fill in some of the details surrounding his death here. He was in jail for murder at the time of his death. The man he killed supposedly called him at his home and told him he was coming to kill him. There had been some type of ongoing dispute between the two. My mom said that Grandpa Oden came to her room, told her goodnight, and said that he loved her. He then went outside, with his rifle, to wait on the man who had threatened him. When the man arrived, my grandfather shot and killed him. He was put on trial for homicide. Despite pleading self-defense, he was convicted of second-degree murder. Between the time of the jury's verdict and his sentencing hearing, my Grandpa Oden was found dead in his jail cell, hanging from a bar above his cell.

Our family never accepted it as a suicide, for several reasons but perhaps most importantly because the person that my grandfather killed had a brother who was in law enforcement. I have been told that the victim's brother was working as a jailer at the time of my grandfather's death. There were also stories from others who were in jail at the time, as well as letters from Grandpa Oden to his family that caused questions to arise concerning the cause of death being a suicide versus a staged suicide. I will never know for sure how my grandfather died, but I do know that his death—whether by his own hand or not—created a horrendous legacy in the community in which his wife (my Nanny) would spend the rest of her life and in which his children (including Momma) would grow up. As I have explained, Monterey is a small town; at the time of my grandfather's death, the population was less than 2,400 residents. Everyone knew everyone else's business. A murder and an apparent jailhouse suicide wouldn't be easily forgotten, and my mother and her siblings would carry the stigma of those events all through their childhoods, into their young adult years, and, at least to some degree, for the rest of their lives.

Even before the homicide, my grandfather didn't have the best reputation. He owned bars and motels, the kind that depended on the business of the more unsavory characters in the area in order to turn a reliable profit. I can't say how deeply involved he was with the criminal element, but I have heard it said that he was involved with the mafia. I'm not sure how true that is, but there is probably at least a nugget of truth to the idea of him being connected to some type of organized crime. At the very least, he had an alcohol problem, possibly a drug problem, and was abusive toward Nanny and Momma.

Nanny had her own troubled past, including giving up two children that she had with another man prior to marrying my grandfather. My grandfather forced her to do so. After my grandfather's death, Nanny got a new boyfriend, and the two of them drank heavily. She may have thought the beer and liquor would help her forget her troubles, but, in truth, it just created more problems. As I have explained earlier, my mother was taken out of Nanny's home for a period of time when she was in high school due to physical abuse. I have also relayed the story of my uncle Nick and his alcoholism and drug addiction. Unfortunately, the third sibling, my aunt Sissy, also developed an alcohol and drug problem during her teen years and young adulthood.

Unlike Uncle Nick, Aunt Sissy managed to keep a job and stay out of legal trouble for several years, despite partying, drinking, and doing drugs on a regular basis. Uncle Nick had regular run-ins with the police over the years, but Aunt Sissy was what one might describe as a "high-functioning addict" for a while. She worked at a home health care center and was a CNA, a certified nurses' aid. She went to various patients' homes to take care of them. She did things like cooking, cleaning, bathing, checking vital signs, and making sure they had taken their medicine. Unfortunately, Aunt Sissy had some personal things happen in her life that caused her substance abuse problem to increase greatly. She was caught drinking and driving, lost her job, and went to rehab.

Around this time, my mom became involved with a guy named Jerry. He wasn't much better than Momma's other boyfriend, Don, had been, but at least Jerry wasn't married. It wasn't very long before Momma and Jerry got married and moved in together. Like Don, Jerry was a heavy drinker. Momma began to drink more regularly, too. Their marriage only lasted about six months, but while they were married, he acted like he owned her and started getting rough with her. He would grab her and push her. She had some bruises from him grabbing her and holding her. I never saw him physically smack her, but I think he did when I wasn't around.

After we moved in with Jerry, I found out that he smoked pot (marijuana). I could smell dope all through our house. Then, one day I walked in and caught them. Momma had been smoking it, too. I threw an absolute fit. I had been taught in school that drugs were bad, and I was shocked and appalled to see my own mother doing something like that. She tried to explain how she didn't do it all the time and didn't have a problem with it. She even offered to let me try it, saying she would rather me try it at home and know I was safe than have me try it on the streets and not know what I was smoking. All I knew about marijuana back then was what I had learned in DARE class at school, and I thought drugs were awful. Needless to say, I did not try smoking pot myself at that time.

This was when a lot of my outbursts of anger resurfaced. I started throwing stuff, hitting walls, and kicking holes in the wall. Now, looking back, I see that I was extremely angry with my mom, but I didn't have the words to explain my feelings at the time. Just like when Daddy left me after my parents divorced, my mother's choices left me feeling rejected and abandoned. I felt she had chosen her husband, alcohol, and drugs over me. I also believed that if she really loved me, she would have quit when I threw a fit. She didn't quit; instead, she continued down a path of destruction that would ultimately threaten both of our lives. The one person I adored and who had always been there for me had disappointed me and let me down, and I didn't know how to act except to get angry. Momma and Jerry were soon separated and divorced. He moved away, and we moved, once again, into an apartment across the road from Nanny.

This is when Momma began working at a beer joint just outside the city limits (Monterey is in the Bible belt, where there were not very many bars, and what bars they did have were called "beer joints" back then for slang). Monterey was in a dry county. By law, there couldn't be any bars inside of the city limits, and they couldn't serve any kind of hard liquor even outside of the city limits. When Momma started working at the bar, she worked the night shift. So, for the most part, I was alone in the evenings. My anger and rage continued to get worse. I thought my mom should be at home with me, not at the bar with these other people, especially men. Even though it was a job, it was not a good job, and I resented her being gone in the evenings. Once, I was talking to her on the phone while she was at work, and the conversation didn't go as I wanted it to, so I threw the phone and busted a hole in the wall.

The phone being thrown into the wall was just one example of the fits I had started throwing. I was really starting to have some major problems with anger and having an even harder time trying to control it. What had begun with me breaking my early childhood caged monkey toy as a little girl had escalated significantly over the years. I began counseling with a psychologist named Dr. Avery. My dad sent extra money to pay for the counseling every month. Dr. Avery came to the conclusion that my outbursts of anger and rage had to do with anger and resentment toward my dad that had never been dealt with or resolved. Somehow, he missed the part about me being mad at my mother for leaving me, figuratively if not literally, in favor of men, alcohol, and marijuana. Maybe I never really told him that part. I think it was easier to use my dad as the scapegoat because he wasn't there physically, even though it was his money paying for my counseling sessions.

I once heard a minister say, "Anything buried alive never dies." That statement is so true! It's like a bad seed has been planted that takes root, sprouts, and continues to grow until it is dealt with and removed, roots and all, or it will sprout and take over. Ultimately, you either deal with it, or it deals with you.

I never would confront my dad about how I had been hurt by the divorce or how I felt about the deterioration of our relationship afterward. I feared that if I told him how I felt, he wouldn't love me anymore. We might not have had a close relationship at that point, but I was clinging to what we had left. Despite all of the years of pain caused by my parents' divorce and my daddy's lack of regular visitation, I still loved my daddy and wanted a relationship with him.

The doctor told me to hit something that wouldn't hurt me and that I couldn't hurt, such as my bed or my pillow, to release my anger and frustration. He said to pretend the object was my dad, but I believe that it's plain to see a lot of my anger was related to my mom and the other men in my mom's life, not just my dad. The anger started with the separation of my parents and the lack of attention and love I received from my dad, but it certainly did not end there.

Deep down, I thought that if my dad had been there, things would have been different. If he had been around, Momma and I wouldn't have been going through all of the turmoil and instability, like these men being mean to Momma, moving every time I turned around, or Momma drinking, using drugs, and having to work and struggle just to get by. I also got attached to some of the men that Momma dated. I desperately needed a father figure in my life, and they were usually good to me even though they weren't so good to her. It seemed like everyone I got attached to left me. Once again, I felt like I had no value and I wasn't important to anyone because if I was important to them, they wouldn't have kept leaving me.

Looking back now, it's obvious there were also generational curses involved in this tragic backstory. The trauma of my parents' divorce and the continuing lack of stability in my life in the years thereafter would have been devastating enough. When combined with the dysfunction on both sides of my family, and the physical, sexual, mental, verbal, and substance abuse of the previous generations, however, I was in a battle that I could never have won on my own (Believe me, I've lost enough family members to know how my own story would have ended had it not been for divine intervention).

Now that you know the situation into which I was born and raised, you may have a better understanding of the desperation of the girl in the cow pasture. That young woman had never known true happiness. What little love she had felt in her life had been from those who were, themselves, too damaged to give her the attention and affection that she craved and deserved. The only real comfort in her life came from drugs and alcohol. They were not good companions, but at least she could depend on them to deliver consistent results.

Fortunately, that young girl's story would eventually change for the better. We'll get to that part in due time (Spoiler alert: with God's help, good can triumph over evil. I'm living proof of it).

Chapter Six

Sex, Drugs, and Rock n' Roll

In my seventh-grade year, we moved back in with Nanny. I believe Momma thought it would help my behavioral problems if I wasn't home alone so much. Due to health problems, Nanny never left home except to go to the doctor or the grocery store, and those were both rare. However, the fact that she was home all the time did not necessarily mean that she would prove to be a good babysitter for me (or an effective disciplinarian when I started to cross the line).

That same school year, my best friend Lori's father died in a car accident. It was an awful, heart-breaking situation, and Lori's family had a really hard time with it. The death was so unexpected, and it took everyone by surprise. Momma let me stay out of school for two weeks to be with Lori since she was struggling so much with her father's death. Attendance policies were not so stringent back then, and I made really good grades; the time out of school didn't negatively affect me academically, but it very well may have negatively affected me in other ways. The school was very small and understanding of situations like that. It was during this time that Lori and I became really close. We had been friends before, but we bonded even more after the accident.

Soon after her dad passed away, Lori and I began experimenting with tobacco, alcohol, and drugs. We were about twelve years old when all this started. We started out stealing our moms' cigarettes. If they noticed, they never said anything to us about it. Then, we progressed to the alcohol that Lori's dad had left behind. He had some Old Charter bourbon whiskey in the kitchen cabinet that he had used to make homemade cough syrup. We snuck and drank some of it every night until we had drunk all of the whiskey and all of the cough syrup. It tasted awful, but we choked it down. The cough syrup was even more disgusting than the bourbon, but they were both nasty. Looking back, I don't really know why we were so determined to go down that particular road. Maybe some of it was curiosity; kids our age were starting to experiment with various things. I'm sure a great deal of it was an attempt to numb the pain of losing Lori's dad, not to mention all the other things we had each gone through in the past. It was, at the very least, a welcome distraction from our day-to-day lives.

I should explain that I, too, had a really hard time with Lori's dad passing. I realize that my own sense of loss was nothing like that of Lori and her family, but it was still really hard for me to accept. He had been a father figure to me—something I didn't have at that time. My mom had dated some guys and had been in some rough relationships, but the only boyfriend of hers who made any attempt to treat me like a daughter was the married guy, and he had been gone for quite some time. My uncle Nick was the closest thing I had to a father figure other than Lori's dad, and that relationship was not at its best due to his drug and alcohol use.

Lori's dad really filled that large, gaping hole in my life for a short period of time. He was like a big teddy bear. He loved to joke with all of us girls. Lori, her sister, several other girls, and I stayed there together sometimes. We would all take turns getting in the recliner with him and sitting in his lap. Lori's sister was older than us. She was fifteen when he passed away, and she would do the same thing, too. When Lori would get in the recliner with him, she would get on one arm of the recliner, and I would get on the other arm. He had nicknames for all of us. He called me C-Baby (I went by Cherie, my middle name, while I lived in Monterey, so that's where the "C" came from). Thinking back on that time brings back a lot of bittersweet memories. It also helps clarify how and why we all started going down the wrong road so quickly after Lori's father died.

Lori's sister had already started experimenting some before her dad passed, but Lori and I had not. Our start into the world of addiction began with our moms' cigarettes and Lori's dad's leftover alcohol. Although I certainly would not advocate for a twelve-year-old to try either of those things, they were relatively innocent compared to what Lori and I were about to get into. Before very long, our lives took a sudden turn from Marlboros and homemade cough syrup to full-blown drug use—and the almost twelve years of full-blown addiction that came with it for me.

The first illegal drug that we tried was LSD (lysergic acid diethylamide, a hallucinogenic drug often referred to as "acid" on the street). That's right; I had my first trip on LSD before I even smoked pot. I'm going to throw a huge disclaimer in here. Don't try this at home. Don't think this is cool or that I am glorifying any of the things I will begin to talk about concerning my downward spiral into addiction because I am not trying to do that at all! However, I do feel that it is necessary to share openly and candidly about those experiences for a couple of reasons. First, if I am to help others who have been there (or are still there), they need to know that I really do understand what they are have been through. I am not someone who took a couple of puffs off of a joint, downed a few pills, and labeled myself as an addict. I lived the life, and I did so for far too many, very miserable years of my youth. Secondly, I believe that I need to help others understand how a life of addiction happens. It's not an overnight thing, and it's not like someone wakes up one day and says, "Oh, I want to grow up to be a 'needle-junkie' someday!" That is not how it happens at all. Sometimes, it does happen fast, as it did with me. Sometimes, it happens gradually, as it did with some others that I know. Either way, it happens every day in this country, on the backroads outside of little tiny towns like where I was raised, to the harsh streets of the inner city, and everywhere in between.

Getting back to the acid story—LSD is not something to play around with. It is a very potent and powerful drug. I was only twelve years old when we "dropped acid" (took LSD) for the first time. Lori and I were at Nanny's house, just hanging out. We both had boyfriends already, and the guys stopped by with some "blotter acid," which means it was paper dipped in LSD. Momma wasn't there. She was at work at the bar. We were at home alone with Nanny and knew we could get away with anything.

Despite the turbulent and sometimes violent physical relationship between Nanny and Momma, Nanny never really even fussed at me or Lori. I guess maybe she had mellowed somewhat over time, but a lot of it was just that she was too disabled and worn out to do very much to us, even if she had been so inclined. It was hard for her to walk, so she mainly just sat in her chair in the living room watching television, venturing only so far as the bathroom and never all the way to the end of the hallway to my bedroom. She would try to call us down every once in a while when we got too loud or when we kept going in and out of the house, but, mostly, she would just tell us to be quiet and to go to my room. Sometimes, she would report our misdeeds to Momma, but that was about as bad as it got. I am certainly not proud of this, but truthfully we mostly ignored Nanny, disregarding what little resistance she gave us and continuing to do whatever we wanted to do—good, bad, or ugly. Now, I know that we were being very disrespectful, but at the time, I had no respect for myself, much less my grandmother. All that I was concerned about was partying and having fun with my friends.

The guys Lori and I were dating at the time, Rick and Josh, were older than us and were already heavy into drugs. My boyfriend's uncle was one of the biggest drug dealers in town, which provided us with access to a wide variety of drugs—and plenty of them. The first time that I smoked pot, I was with my boyfriend and his cousin. There we were, walking down the road, smoking weed in broad daylight. We were even passing it around, which would have made it obvious to anyone paying attention that it was a joint and not a regular cigarette! How we didn't get busted by the police is beyond me, but this became our norm. We didn't see the dangers in what we were doing. It's like we thought we were invisible or invincible, maybe both. Young and immature, yes, I'm sure that was part of it. The other thing was the drugs themselves; part of their effect was to give us a false illusion that no one else knew what was going on.

Before long, Lori and I had started smoking cigarettes and pot on a regular basis. The first time I ever got busted by Momma for smoking cigarettes was at Nanny's house. I had burned a hole in my bedroom window screen with a cigarette so that we could blow our smoke out the window and put our ashes and cigarette butts through the hole. I thought I was really smart, but I never thought to pick up all the cigarette butts that were piling up in front of the house. That sounds really stupid now, but it shows how young and foolish I was and how I didn't really think things through (I wasn't even officially a teenager yet).

The next time I got busted by Momma, I was walking down the road puffing away when she rolled up behind me in her car and caught me red-handed. After I got caught that time, Momma started smelling my breath. I thought I could outsmart her, so I started chewing gum to cover my breath. Then, she started smelling my fingers, so she still got me! She had been there, done that, and knew how to get me before I got one over on her.

My mother's trust wasn't the only thing I lost during that time. The year that I was twelve, I also lost my virginity to my fourteen-year-old boyfriend. We were far from alone; sex usually goes hand in hand with alcohol and drugs. Josh and I dated for about two years, and I thought it was love. When you're young, it's very easy to think that you are in love with someone and that you are going to be together forever. You don't think about the future or the consequences of your actions. You don't think about how other people will look at you or treat you. You don't think about the dangers of your actions or the possibility that you may not like yourself later on because of what you have given up. All you can think of is that if you don't give yourself to this boy that you care so much about, he won't love you and won't stay with you. Later, you will regret losing your innocence at such a young age, but you can't go back and change it. Oftentimes you just keep repeating the same behaviors and patterns, trying to fill those holes and voids created by rejection and abandonment—looking for love in all the wrong places, sex, drugs, and all that goes along with them.

Around the age of thirteen, Lori and I were introduced to a variety of pills. V-cut, blue Valium "nerve pills" quickly became our favorite.

We snorted and took so many valiums that we both got severe kidney infections and began to pass blood. At the age of fourteen, we tried cocaine for the first time, and we both fell in love! Cocaine is a stimulant and is extremely addictive. We started out cleaning our moms' houses to get money for cocaine. Then, we started stealing money when that wasn't enough anymore. Cocaine is so addictive; it's unreal! We could never get enough. Unlike relationships and thinking I was in love with my boyfriend, cocaine became something I really couldn't live without. I did some crazy things in relationships out of fear of losing the person I thought I was "in love" with, but that was nothing compared to what I would do for drugs.

We already had a problem with Valium. Our drug addiction began there, but cocaine took things to a completely different level. It was no longer all "fun and games," so to speak. We blasted past the teenage experimentation phase in which we were only borderline addicted to pills, pot, and alcohol and quickly transitioned into full-blown drug addicts. Lying and stealing to get coke or other drugs meant nothing to us. At just fourteen years old, we were already at a level of addiction that many adult recreational drug users never even reach. We were no longer in control. Instead, *drugs* were beginning to control *us*.

From my own experience, and from what I have seen with many others, when someone first starts using drugs, it is just something to do—a pastime, so to speak. Maybe it's a game; it might seem exciting or like the cool thing to do to fit in. It may provide a temporary numbing for some type of emotional pain. In the beginning, most people can pretty much take it or leave it. Although there are exceptions, there is a time period during which most people have the power to walk away if it doesn't suit them. Soon, however, the excitement, the emotional escape, or whatever fleeting thing it was that lured the person into the world of drugs fades away, and true addiction sets it. From there on, it is extremely difficult to break free.

Addiction is a very vicious cycle. The person who becomes addicted has to use more and more of the substance to get the same feeling, but no matter how much they use, they never really reach the high they are looking for. That's why addiction is so hard to break. It's like you are searching for something that is right in front of you, but you can't touch it. There are even different terms that are commonly used in the drug world to define what I'm talking about. The one I heard most was "chasing the train." It's like you can see the train, but you can never catch the train. The vision of the train is constantly tormenting you. Another analogy is a horse with a carrot tied out in front of it. The horse cannot actually reach the carrot to eat it, but the horse doesn't know that; therefore, the horse will do whatever you tell it to do because it thinks it will get the carrot as a reward. That's how I felt when I was a drug addict: like the elusive, mystical, perfect high that I craved was right in front of me but, try as I might, I could not reach it.

Lori and I continued to use more and more drugs as we chased the train of our addiction, and we began to hang out with a lot of older people. This is when Lori started dating a guy named Lloyd, and I dated a friend of his who was ten years older than me (I was still in my early teens, but he was well into his twenties). Lori and Lloyd became serious and settled down for a while. I, on the other hand, entered a very wild phase, dating several guys who were much older than me (statutory rape was the least of our concerns). As I had been doing in one form or another for most of my life, I searched for someone who would truly love me. Unfortunately, I was looking in all the wrong places and finding nothing. I guess that, in a way, love was just another train that I was chasing during that time.

Chapter Seven

On the Hunt

After Lori and Lloyd became serious, I started hanging out with a girl named Leanne. She was a few years older than me and had her own vehicle. At the time, Leanne was dating a guy a few years older than her. His name was Matt, and his two best friends were Brad and Stephen. We all hung out and ran around together a lot back then.

In the summer of 1995, one particular summer day, we all ended up at the city park, just hanging out and partying a little. There was a whole group of kids there that day drinking and partying, not just our usual group of five. Leanne wasn't really a partier, though, and I don't remember her drinking that day. In fact, she very rarely did anything back then. She may have tried alcohol and maybe a little other stuff, but that was about it. She just liked to hang out with all of us who did party.

I, on the other hand, was a different story. I was a mess. I always used, and that day was no different than any other day. When I got to the park, I tried to get some beer from my friend, Stephen, but he wouldn't give me any. He told me I was too young, and he said that he wasn't "contributing" to me. I was just fourteen, and he was nineteen. Legally, he could've gotten in trouble for contributing to the delinquency of a minor. Even though he wasn't of legal drinking age either, he was an adult, and I wasn't. Still, I believe it was more than that for him. Stephen was a great guy with a really good heart, and I don't think he wanted to see me ruin my life with alcohol and drugs, but I didn't understand that then. I argued with him about it because I wasn't used to not getting what I wanted, no matter how young I was.

Since there were several other people at the park, I ended up getting what I wanted anyway. I drank some Jim Beam and smoked some weed with some of the other people who were there. Then the five of us—Leanne, Matt, Brad, Stephen, and I—decided to go to Cookeville, a larger town about fifteen minutes away, to try out the new Taco Bell. It was the night of their grand opening. On the way, Stephen asked us to drop him off at the local game room, but we talked him into riding to Cookeville with us. The decision to pressure him into going along with us would haunt the other four of us for many years.

As we passed by the game room where Stephen had asked to be dropped off, we were listening to a Lynyrd Skynyrd cassette tape in the car. When the song "On the Hunt" came on, out of the blue, Stephen said he wanted that song played at his funeral. What an odd thing for a teenager to say. Little did we know we know that, in a matter of days, we would be attending Stephen's funeral and, despite his family's objections, playing that very song as we drove to his graveside.

As we headed out of town, we got onto the interstate to take the short drive to Cookeville. When we were almost to our exit, the driver looked away from the road and began messing with the radio. We were headed straight for the guardrail, and I freaked out. I was sitting in the front seat, so I started screaming, panicked, and grabbed the steering wheel. We hit the guardrail anyway, and the car flipped over. We then slid across the road and struck the other guardrail, flipped again, and slid back across the road. When it was over, we were back at the first guardrail, upside down, facing back toward Monterey.

The song "On the Hunt" was still playing on the car stereo when we crashed. Despite all the damage to the car, the song was still blaring out of the speakers as we began to get out of the car. I have no idea how I got out, but I was the first one who was able to get out of the car. Matt and Brad then got out on their own, and they helped Leanne out. There was no movement from Stephen. Matt and Brad tried to pull Stephen out from the passenger side window, but he was a big guy, and they couldn't get him out. Even if they had been able to free him from the vehicle, it was too late. He was gone. His head and face were mangled, his head was busted open, and brain matter was seeping out. We were all in shock and absolutely hysterical. A nurse who was traveling that way stopped to try and help us and calm us down. She's the one who told us Stephen was already gone and called for help for the rest of us.

We were all taken to the hospital. None of us was severely injured. The guys had a few scrapes. Leanne had a concussion and stitches in her foot. I had a concussion, a cracked jaw bone, stitches in my chin, staples in my right knee, and damaged cartilage in my left knee. When Momma got to the hospital, I had two or three packs of cigarettes in my flannel shirt pockets. She felt so sorry for me and was just so glad I was alive that she let me smoke in front of her for the first time. Later that same night, Momma tried to tell me that God had saved me for a reason, but I couldn't see it. I was just devastated that Stephen was gone.

We all attended Stephen's funeral service. Even though we were not exactly "welcomed" by his family, they did not ask us to leave, either. Of course, they blamed us for the accident and for Stephen's death. I'm sure I would have felt the same way if I had been in their shoes.

No one could have blamed us any more than we blamed ourselves, though. It's an awful feeling to think you caused or were even part of a friend's death. It was hard to understand why we made it, why we survived, and why Stephen didn't. After the wreck, I would often go through my mom's apartment screaming and crying out, "Why didn't I die instead of him? I wish I would've died." It was awful. I really hated myself. I really, seriously wanted to die. I was sincere when I would scream and say that I would have it rather been me instead of him. I couldn't live with the guilt of surviving and him not making it. It would have been bad enough just knowing that four of us walked away from an accident that took our friend's life, but it was devastating to know that he had wanted to stay in Monterey and that we had talked him into going with us anyway. Even worse, I found out that, because of the way the wreck had happened, Stephen had saved my life. He had literally covered me and protected me during the impact.

This all makes me think of that old Randy Travis song, "Three Wooden Crosses." The song is about a wreck involving a farmer, a teacher, a preacher, and a hooker. The farmer, teacher, and preacher died in the crash, but the hooker survived. That seems backward to the outcome most of us would think ideal, but, according to the song, three of them had something good to leave behind here on earth and were prepared to die. The hooker, on the other hand, would have died lost in sin, gone to hell, and left nothing good behind. I can certainly relate to the hooker in that song. After the wreck, she ended up with the preacher's blood-stained Bible. She turned her life around, surrendered her life to the Lord, and raised her son reading that blood-stained Bible. Her son became a preacher and was the one telling the story of the three wooden crosses in a sermon, one for each of those killed in the wreck, while using that same blood-stained Bible. I had nothing good to leave behind at that time, and I certainly was not ready to leave this life. By contrast, Stephen was very special in many ways and was not living like the rest of us.

At the funeral, the family wouldn't allow us to play the "On the Hunt" song that Stephen had said he wanted played at his funeral just minutes before his death. So, instead, we followed the funeral procession and played it as loud as the stereo would go, repeatedly, all the way to the graveyard. At the time, we thought that's what he would have wanted. Now, I see that was extremely disrespectful, but we were young and thought we were following his wishes.

It was sometime after the funeral that Momma took Leanne and me to the lot where the car had been towed, and that's when I truly realized Stephen's death had saved my life. I had been sitting in the front passenger seat, and he was sitting directly behind me. The initial impact threw me into the floorboard and threw him partially out of my passenger side window. The metal rod in the back of my seat was permanently bent down from his body weight.

Like I said earlier, I don't know how I got out of the vehicle. By looking at the car, it would have been almost impossible for me to get out on my own. My head hit the windshield, my chin hit the dash, and my knees were on the floorboard. I had been wedged into a position of safety. There was blood all over the car, and my hair was on the windshield. The tow truck driver told us that if Stephen had not pushed my seat down with the weight of his body, I would probably have flown out of the windshield and been killed.

This is when I really started losing it and blaming myself. It just continued to get worse. I would just go all to pieces and scream and cry, saying, "Why didn't I die instead of him? I wish I would've died." I really meant it, too. I really didn't want to live at that point because I felt so guilty. I felt like it should have been me instead of him. I truly wished that I would have died instead of Stephen. If only we had not talked him into going with us! I blamed myself because I grabbed the steering wheel. I felt like it was my fault because I had asked him to go. After the wreck, my mom found out from his mom he had a secret crush on me. That made me feel even worse because I felt that, because he had liked me, I had been more responsible for persuading him than the others.

I would never admit it back then, but I blamed the others, too. I believe that was all rooted in my own guilt. It took some of the guilt and pressure off of me; if I put some of the blame on someone else, at least we could share the blame instead of me feeling it was all my fault. Today, I don't blame anyone. You can't blame anyone for something like that. It was exactly what it is called: an accident, a car accident. That's what it was. No one ever meant for anyone to get hurt. No one had any ill intentions.

Another reason that it was hard for all of us to deal with the wreck was that we felt like everyone looked at us like murderers as if we had purposefully killed our friend. Leanne especially had a hard time with it because it was her vehicle. The authorities put us all under investigation, but there were never any charges filed.

I had so many mixed emotions stirring inside because of the wreck. I was sad, I was angry, I felt terribly guilty. I think I had a little of every emotion possible and a whole lot of some. This is when I had started counseling with a new psychologist. When I first started working with her, I couldn't remember very many details of what had happened in the accident. I knew we had wrecked, of course, and that Stephen was gone, but the details were fuzzy in the beginning. I remembered going toward the guardrail and grabbing the steering wheel, but I didn't remember anything else until the point at which I was out of the car. Even some of that I could not fully remember at first. The counselor said my mind was protecting me against things that, mentally and emotionally, I couldn't handle. I was taught different relaxation techniques, and by the end of the therapy sessions, I was able to remember almost everything about the wreck except how I got out of the car.

    I still, to this day, do not know how I got out of the car, but I do believe God somehow brought me out. I have even wondered if an angel brought me out of the car, especially when I think back about what the man who hauled the car away said. There was no reasonable explanation for me to be able to get out of the car on my own with the way my seat was wedged down, and there is definitely not a natural explanation for me to have been the first one out of the car without another human being there to help get me out. Somehow, for some reason, I made it out. Maybe someone out there needed to hear my story—all of my story, not just the tragedy.

I love you and miss you "Stephen." You are gone but never forgotten. Your memory, life, and impact never taken for granted.

Chapter Eight

Momma's Sick and I'm Out of Control

After the wreck, my life continued to go downhill. The addiction got worse. I couldn't use enough to forget about what had happened—my parents' divorce, not having my dad in my life, my mom's erratic, abusive behavior, the wreck... No matter what I used or tried mixing together, those haunting memories never went completely away. My home life was awful. Not only was *I* mentally unstable after the wreck, but my mom became mentally unstable, too. She had had trouble with anxiety and nervousness since I was a small child, but as I got older, she also became depressed, and the nervousness became worse. Momma was eventually diagnosed with bipolar disorder, also known as manic depressive disorder. I was around fourteen, which would have made her thirty-two years old at the time of her diagnosis. This happened within a year of the wreck in which my friend Stephen died.

For anyone who doesn't understand, bipolar disorder can cause extreme emotional highs and lows. It's like living on an emotional roller coaster. There's a real lack of emotional stability, and it's not the person's fault. Lots of times, the fluctuation is due to a chemical imbalance. According to the doctors, this was my mom's situation. The doctors tried several different medications to try to stabilize her.

The medications would work for a while, but the effects never lasted long enough to truly help her—to truly help us. The doctors always had to increase her dosage or change her medication altogether. It was as if her body developed an immunity to each new medication that the doctor prescribed.

Oh, how I hated and resented my mother's mental illness! I didn't hate Momma herself, but there were many times that I took out my anger over her condition on her. I regret my actions now, but I didn't understand it then. I didn't get how my mother's mental illness could make her want to stay in bed all the time instead of spending time with me. I can vividly remember her bedroom. By that time, we had moved out of Nanny's house and were living in public housing—in the projects. Our apartment had off-white walls and old, speckled crème tile on the floor. Momma still had the bedroom suite from when she and my dad were together. It was a nice wooden bedroom set with a nightstand, a dresser, and a chest of drawers. She had a solid pinkish-looking comforter. I think it was considered "mauve," actually, which was a popular decorating color at the time. That comforter is what I remember most because that's mostly what I saw whenever I tried to interact with her.

She would just go get in the bed and pull the comforter completely over her head. She was probably trying to disappear from the world, I now realize, or maybe hide from it. I would leave home in the morning, telling her goodbye through the comforter. I would go to school and come home to her still covered up in that bed. I would be so mean to her sometimes because I didn't understand. I would throw fits and throw temper tantrums. Eventually, I would just leave her, still cowering under that comforter, and go get high.

Now, I understand that Momma was suffering from a serious mental illness. Back then, however, I thought that she just didn't love me enough to get up and spend time with me. As is usually the case with manic-depressives, there was another, even darker side to my mother's illness. She didn't stay in bed with her head covered all the time. Sometimes, the pendulum would swing, and she would flip out on me and become verbally and physically abusive. Then, when her mental state headed back in the other direction, she would sometimes become suicidal. As a young teenager, I didn't have the capacity to understand why my mother would lose her temper and fly off the handle and get abusive with me, and I definitely didn't comprehend what caused her to want to take her own life and leave me all alone in the world. She would tell me that I was all she had and that I was her whole world; if those things were true, how could she want to take her life and leave me behind?

When I think back on it now, I think maybe Momma just wanted to escape or to run away. In her mind, perhaps she thought the world, including me, would be better off without her. What she couldn't see was that she was also my world and my role model. Yeah, she may have had some faults, as we all do, and some serious issues, as many do, but I loved her. She was my momma, and she meant everything to me. All I saw were her good qualities, most of all that she loved me no matter what, and that she was always there for me when she wasn't sick. She was my momma! I loved her dearly, and I still do. She was a great person with a great heart, one of the best, sweetest people I have ever met in my life when she was well. I've heard many people say the same thing about her, including my husband. Of course, not everyone saw the other side of her—the side where the mental illness had tried to destroy her, her personality, her mind, and even her life.

When I was between the age of fourteen and fifteen, there were two separate occasions when Momma actually attempted suicide. The first time, she took a bunch of her prescription medications, which included antidepressants, mood stabilizers, nerve pills, and sleeping pills. The day this happened, I came home from school and found her in her bedroom crying and really upset. Once we started talking, she told me what she had done. I started crying, too, and screaming hysterically for her to gag herself and vomit up the pills. I didn't want to lose my momma! I didn't know what I would do without her or if I could even survive without her. After pleading with her, I was finally able to get her to go to the bathroom and gag herself until she threw up. She vomited quite a bit of the medication back up, but a lot of it had already made it into her bloodstream. The effects of the medication were starting to show, so I called 911 for help. An ambulance came to get her, and she was hospitalized in a mental health facility.

A few months later, the second time that Momma attempted to kill herself, it was even worse. Similar scenario, I came in from school, but this time I found her under that pink comforter on her bed. She was still alive, but she was not well at all. She had ingested all of her prescription medication and had put nicotine patches all over her body. For those who don't know, too much nicotine can actually kill you, and that's what she was trying to do. Because of what had happened with her first suicide attempt, she took greater efforts to end things the second time. Her intention was to be dead and gone before I got home from school and found her. It didn't work out that way; she was still breathing when I got there. I didn't waste any time calling 911. Momma was hospitalized again.

● ● ●

During her hospitalization, Momma was very unsatisfied with the care that she was given at the facility. Consequently, she wrote a seven-page letter to the office of administration about how she thought things needed to be done differently (In case you have forgotten, my mother was a very smart woman—a would-have-been valedictorian—before that fateful night in which Nanny beat her so severely that she chose to head out into a snowstorm and start hitchhiking rather than spend another minute at home). After Momma stabilized and was released from the facility, the mental health center gave her a job in the exact position that she had written the letter about. Momma seemed to do a lot better after that.

I had not seen my mother do that well mentally in years. I believe the fact that she was working to help other people with similar problems helped her tremendously. Maybe she felt like she was finally doing something right, something positive, and was making a difference in others' lives. I, on the other hand, was definitely not helping her mental state in any way. Given how I was behaving at the time, Momma must have felt like she was a failure as a mother. She would often tell me as much when she would get down and out, especially when we were arguing. I'm sure she felt helpless and hopeless as a single mother, dealing with mental illness and working while trying to raise a rebellious, out of control, teenage girl.

The first big blow-up that sticks out in my mind after her release from the hospital that second time was when she caught me, for the first time, doing something other than just smoking cigarettes. I was around fourteen or fifteen at the time. My boyfriend and another guy had been at my mom's apartment drinking and smoking pot on the back porch. They forgot and left their rolling papers and a can of beer outside on the kitchen window pane. The next morning, Momma was at the sink washing dishes. When she looked out the window, she saw the beer can and rolling papers. I was still in bed at the time. Needless to say, I got a rude awakening from Momma that morning. Then, she called my daddy.

This was the first time my mom had ever caught me with anything other than cigarettes. At that time, Momma didn't know about any of my previous drug use. Despite my blatant disregard for toeing the line over the past two or three years, my mother had somehow remained oblivious to my pot-smoking, valium-popping, coke-snorting ways until she saw that beer can on the window sill. Right away, she called my dad at work and told him what had happened. He freaked out and offered to come back home to live with us.

Like lots of other children of divorce, I had always wanted my mom and dad to get back together. As I have talked about previously, I had spent many years longing for my father to be a regular part of my life again. I desperately longed for his love and his presence in my life. However, once I had the actual chance to get what I had always thought I wanted—that ideal, perfect family life—I didn't want it anymore. It wasn't because I didn't still want my daddy in my life; it was because I knew that I would have to straighten up if I had both my parents watching over me. Looking back at the situation now, it makes me see how strongly drugs and alcohol had already gotten ahold of me.

For years, I had longed for a relationship with my daddy. I thought I wanted that more than anything else in the world, and when I was younger, I did. By the time that my parents were willing to come together again for my sake, it was too late. At that point, I wanted drugs more than I wanted my family back together. Although my daddy finally showed me that he loved me enough to leave his life and everything he had behind in order to help save mine, I simply didn't love myself enough to do the same.

• • •

So, nothing changed. Daddy stayed where he was, and we continued down a slow road of death and destruction, and this is how it continued. Momma ended up with another guy. She started dating Terry, who was a severe alcoholic who took my friend Kayla and me to get some vodka at the bootlegger's place. Mind you, I was still between fourteen and fifteen at this time, and Kayla was the same age as me. Monterey was a dry county where liquor could not be sold legally anywhere; that's why we had "bootleggers" who sold liquor illegally. Once Terry got us the liquor from the bootlegger, we mixed it with grapefruit juice and got absolutely wasted. Even though we were severely intoxicated, Terry's driving scared us because he was driving like a maniac. He even got *on* the *off*-ramp of the interstate, going the wrong direction. Finally, we got him drop us off at the city park, and we walked over to the home of Kayla's boyfriend, Todd.

I got sick as a dog almost as soon as we got there. It was absolutely disgusting. I missed the toilet and was lying in my own vomit on the bathroom floor. I had not only puked all over myself and the bathroom floor, but I had also urinated all over myself because I was too drunk to get up off of the floor. It was so nasty. I hate to even share this. Of course, I can only share bits and pieces of my life according to what I feel God wants me to share because there is so much, as is with everyone's life. This just happens to be one of those things that God strangely led me to share. Maybe it's because you would think lying on the bathroom floor with my face in vomit and my body soaked in my own urine would be the lowest point in my life, but it wasn't. Not at all, not even close. I wasn't done trying to destroy myself yet, not by a long shot.

Todd came to the bathroom to see if I was alright, but I just cried, "I want my momma." So, he called her. This shows that I was still just a baby in a sense, even though I thought I was all grown up and could do whatever I wanted. When Momma came to get me, she asked me where I got the alcohol, and I told her the truth. She found a vodka bottle in her car, so she took it inside and beat Terry with it. I don't think she really hurt him because he was too messed up to feel much of anything. Momma didn't hit me that night. I guess she knew she didn't need to. I was being punished enough for what I had done. I was so sick. I truly believe I had alcohol poisoning, which is potentially fatal.

Between the wreck and this incident, Momma gave in and let me start partying at home. I was about fifteen, and she was about 33 when we started partying together. She thought, this way, she would at least know where I was, that I was okay, and whether I was dead or alive. It wasn't long before my friends, and I had her smoking pot and partying with us. Granted, she had partied some in the past, but it had never really become a habit for her until she started getting high with us.

She had been in a couple of car wrecks previously and was dealing with some physical pain. The first wreck happened when she was driving our car; she pulled out from a stop sign, and a full-size truck hit her in the side. In the second wreck, she was with Terry. He was drinking and driving and ran them over a cliff. It's a miracle they weren't hurt any worse than they were. He didn't get hurt because he was so intoxicated he wasn't expecting the impact. His body was limp instead of bracing for impact, so the wreck did less damage to him than it might otherwise have done. Momma was hurt pretty bad, though. Her collar bone was broken, and her shoulder was messed up. She lost over 90 percent use of her right hand, and she was right-handed.

The doctors had her on pain medication, but we thought we had the best pain killer of all—marijuana! This was back in the 1990s when studies were starting to come out saying how much smoking pot could help cancer patients with their pain. So, that's the logic we used to get her to join in. Like they say, "If you can't beat 'em, join 'em." Well, that's what she did.

This is when I started dating Toby, my friend Todd's cousin. He was ten or eleven years older than me. He had a good job and a car, but he had a really bad habit, too. He kept and smoked a lot of weed, but his biggest addiction was crack cocaine. Crack cocaine is plain old cocaine that has been cooked down so you can smoke it. It is so addictive, it's just unreal. The actual high is really strong but only lasts for a few seconds, leaving the user unfulfilled and continuously chasing that high. I was back to "chasing that train."

Toby moved in with me at Momma's apartment. He kept Momma in weed, and it kept her happy. She didn't really know what was going on with us and the crack. We started out smoking a little crack in the evening after he got off work. Then, we would go to the house and smoke weed until we chilled out enough to go to bed.

We started hanging out at the dealer's house a lot. This was the same dealer I mentioned very early on, my ex-boyfriend's uncle. He was one of the biggest drug dealers in Monterey. We would buy a little ourselves and smoke it with the dealer and his wife. Then, they would match us. It always just went from there. None of us could stop, not if there was any way to keep from it. I have no idea how Toby didn't lose his job or how I didn't flunk out of high school during that time. Yes, I was still in high school—still in my mid-teens.

It was really hard to go to school paranoid from the after-effects of partying all night and even harder to get through the day once the dope was all gone. I would be sitting there in class, going through withdrawals. It was a miserable existence, but at the time, I thought I was living the life.

Thank God, those days are over. Always chasing something but never being satisfied is a terrible way to live. Toby and I didn't stay together too long because of the drug use. His addiction to crack was getting worse and worse. I did slow down on the crack after we split up, but I didn't slow down partying in general.

Chapter Nine

I Said, "No!"

One night, I was just sitting around the house with Momma and Larry, her best friend who was a bad alcoholic. He was drinking beer, but we were out of weed. I was bored and definitely not satisfied with beer. I talked them into taking me out riding around to see if I could find somebody to get out and party with. I couldn't find anyone in town, so we rode out to the bar called the "Hot Spot," where I ran into "Dog" and Junior. I got in the car with them, and Momma went back home. Dog was about my uncle Nick's age, at least ten years older than me. He had been friends with my uncle for years. I guess Momma thought he could be trusted, but that was far from the truth.

Dog and Junior had blue valiums and vodka, so I was more than happy to go hang out with them. They were both messed up when I got in the car. I was fifteen, so it didn't take me long to get messed up, too. We rode around and partied until we ran out of gas a few miles outside of town. Junior lived in one direction, and Dog and I lived in the other direction.

We parted ways. Dog and I started walking to his house, and Junior walked to his house. Somebody picked us up and took us to Dog's house. Dog had told me to stay at his house until daylight, and he would borrow his grandma's truck to take me home. He lived in a little cabin in the eyesight of his grandma's house. I knew him and his grandmother fairly well. I had been to his cabin partying several times, so I didn't think anything of it. I thought I would be okay. I didn't see any danger, but as soon as we were alone in his cabin, he started trying to kiss me. At first, I didn't react very much. I thought he would quit. I was wrong. He just kept on. I started resisting, and he got forceful. I said "no" and told him to stop, but he wouldn't. He started going further. I still kept telling him no and to stop, but he didn't. He kept going until he raped me, and then he passed out.

I stayed up all night. I never went to sleep because I was so upset. I was scared, but I was more in shock than anything. I went numb. I never cried or anything; I just waited until daylight and started trying to wake him up. It took a while for me to get him to come to. When I finally got him to wake up, we went to his grandma's. She fixed us breakfast, we ate with her, and he took me home like nothing had ever happened, but something had happened. I had been violated, forced into doing something I did not want to do, with someone that I did not want to be with in that way.

Something inside of me was dying, yet I was numb at the same time. I just shut down. I didn't do it on purpose. I didn't know what I was feeling or how to react, so instead of reacting in an appropriate manner, I sat at a table and ate toast with my rapist and his grandmother like nothing unusual had taken place the night before. Emotionally, I just blocked it all out, kind of like I did with the details of the wreck when Stephen died. I never *tried* to block anything out. It just happened. Somehow, unintentionally, in my mind, I had stopped the thoughts and feelings to keep from experiencing things emotionally that I couldn't handle. I had some thoughts and emotions, of course, but somehow, I turned them off.

Nobody had a clue what Dog had done to me. I told Momma about us running out of gas and how I had to stay at his house, but I did not tell her about the rape. Somewhere in my mind, I thought that if I didn't talk about it, then it didn't really happen—like I could ignore it, and it would go away. I am not sure whether Dog even remembered what had happened. He didn't act like he remembered anyway, and I was too afraid, ashamed, and embarrassed to say anything about it. I felt like it was my fault because I had been out partying with him—a teenage girl out with a man well into his twenties.

I can only imagine how girls feel who get date-raped. Maybe you were okay with a little kissing and cuddling, but when he wanted to go further, and you said no, he didn't listen. Yes, I put myself in an extremely unsafe situation, but when someone says no, it means NO, not maybe, or just go ahead, and we'll act like it never happened. No means NO! Absolutely not! Do not hurt me! Do not touch me! Do not in any way harm me or violate me or my space! No matter what the situation is, rape is never, ever the victim's fault. I know that now. I didn't know that back then.

I didn't tell anyone about the rape for over a year. Lori's mom took me, Lori, and another friend of ours to Myrtle Beach the summer after Dog forced himself on me. I finally confided in them about what had happened. It was humiliating to tell them because, to me, this guy was not in any way appealing. If he was at least attractive to me, maybe I could have played it off, at least in my own mind. I know that sounds sick, but it's true. Lori told me that if I didn't tell Momma, she was going to.

When we got back home, I sat down and told Momma the whole story. She was furious. First, she wanted to go to the cops, but I said no. I didn't want to relive it all over again. Plus, there was no evidence other than my word. Then, she decided she would kill him. She was convinced that she could get away with it because he lived way out in the boonies. Even if she did get caught, she was so furious at the moment that she really didn't care if she went to jail or not. She finally calmed down when she saw that I needed her to be there for me instead of locked away in jail for killing Dog. I also had her promise me she would never tell Uncle Nick. I was afraid of what he might do, and he was already in enough trouble with the law.

After all that, I started hanging out with some new people, Shelley and Ben. They were a few years older than me and worked at the same local bar. Shelley was my next-door neighbor. She and Ben were tight, mainly because Ben was getting ounces of cocaine from out of state. There was a lot of dealing going on at the apartments. I helped out in the evenings while they were at work, and they kept me high in return. Everybody got high at the bar, too, but they were afraid to carry much dope on them to work. It was not only a "Hot Spot" for partying and dope but also for the cops.

We not only did a lot of coke (cocaine), but we also smoked a lot of pot, tripped on 'shrooms (psilocybin mushrooms, a hallucinogen known as "magic mushrooms") quite a few times, and got on crank (methamphetamine) pretty bad. I was on anything and everything I could get my hands on. I even took over-the-counter speed pills called "two-ways" that were stimulants.

Dog, the guy who raped me, was one of our biggest go-to guys. He could get crank for us from people we didn't know. I went to his house, got high with him, and went places with him like nothing had ever happened. I told Shelley what had transpired between him and me and made it a point to never be alone with him after the rape, but this is a prime example of what drugs do to you. Despite the ongoing trauma of the rape, I was willing to be around my rapist just to get high. Over and over again, I was willing to put myself in dangerous and compromising situations in order to keep on chasing that ever-elusive train of drug addiction.

Honestly, I didn't want to be without my drugs, but I also didn't want to be rejected. In other words, I not only wanted to stay high, but I also wanted to be accepted by all of my partying buddies. Most of them were at least five to ten years older than me, which made me feel much more grown-up than I actually was. People my age couldn't normally get as much of the hard stuff like crank and cocaine, but that's what I wanted and what I was used to. I didn't want to feel like I was a danger to my older friends because I was underage. I heard the term "jailbait" enough. Most of the older people wouldn't even hang out with people my age because they were afraid of getting in trouble.

Everybody let me in, though, because they knew my family, my highly dysfunctional and very notorious family. Because of my uncle Nick, my aunt Sissy, my nanny Jimmie Mae, my momma, and probably even my grandfather and some of my extended family, the ones I partied with knew I was "cool" and wouldn't run my mouth or get them in trouble. The term "cool" here does not mean fashionable or hip. It means they could trust me not to be a "snitch" (a slang term for a confidential informant for the police). At the time, it seemed like a good thing. I thought that being cool worked in my favor, but now I see that it was a curse and not a blessing.

I'm not saying I was "all that," but my looks didn't hurt either. It helped being a young, pretty, outgoing girl in the party scene. However, being a young, pretty girl can be a very dangerous thing in the wrong hands—including my own. The whole social scene of using was really important to me. I wanted to fit in and have a good time. I was always the fun party girl. That was my personality. I was always up for a good time. I loved that life for a period of time, but it nearly killed me. It did kill me spiritually for many years, but also almost killed me mentally, emotionally, and physically.

Chapter Ten

When Suicide Becomes an Option

I started getting strung out really bad, especially on cocaine and crank. I did it all and loved it all, but the cocaine and crank were really getting ahold of me. I started having all kinds of mental, emotional, and physical issues. I was fifteen. Momma thought all of my problems were coming from anxiety, but my biggest problem was addiction. Still, no one saw it, or, if they did, no one addressed it. I don't think that Momma knew the full extent of my drug use. Yes, she knew I drank and smoked a little weed, but I had learned to hide the heavier drug use fairly well. All Momma knew to do was take me to the doctor. She sent me back to mental health counseling and took me to a general physician.

The physician diagnosed me with various stomach problems, including the starting of ulcers. The psychologist and psychiatrist diagnosed me with post-traumatic stress disorder, anxiety disorder, and mild depression. I believe most of my problems stemmed from drug abuse and the fact that I had never fully dealt with the wreck or the rape and had not even begun to touch the surface of the issues I had with my parents. I did have all the problems they said that I had and probably more, but much of it was drug-induced. My stomach stayed tore up from partying and not eating. Of course, I couldn't sleep and had anxiety—my favorite drug was speed. Any drug, especially speed, can cause depression and mood swings. Drug abuse causes your emotions to be all over the place. When you are high, you feel one way. When you don't have enough, you feel another way. When you're running out, you feel yet another way. When you're going through withdrawals, you feel like you're dying. And, too, there was the stress of trying to keep my drug addiction and hard-partying ways a secret from my mother and other family members (and the legal authorities, of course).

The doctors didn't know I was using illegal drugs, so they simply treated my presenting symptoms in the best way they knew how. The physician put me on all kinds of stomach medicine, and the psychiatrist put me on Prozac, Buspar, Lorazepam, and Trazadone. Prozac was prescribed for depression, Buspar was prescribed to stabilize my moods, Trazadone was prescribed to help me sleep at night, and Lorazepam was prescribed for anxiety.

The day after the psychiatrist put me on all of that medicine, I went to school and had a complete breakdown. The illegal drugs, of course, exacerbated my problems, but the diagnosis was what triggered the mental breakdown. As I have already discussed, I hated my mother's mental illness, and now they were saying I was mentally ill, too. I thought it meant I was crazy. I couldn't accept being labeled with multiple mental illnesses. I just couldn't take it and thought I would be better off dead.

I went into the school bathroom and had a complete meltdown. I was hysterical. I threatened to kill myself and tore one of the bathroom stall doors off its hinges. The school secretary came to the bathroom and calmed me down. She was so sweet, kind, and understanding. She shared how she had suffered from depression and had had thoughts of suicide in the past. I see now how God placed her there that very day to help me. We never know when or how God will use us to minister to someone else. It may not have fully sunk in that day, but a seed of hope had been sown. I knew she was a good Christian woman, and I remember her kindness all these years later. She stayed with me and kept me calm until my mom could get to me.

My mom was still working at Plateau Mental Health Center at that time, so she and her boss picked me up and drove me to Nashville, where I was hospitalized. Due to a problem that occurred at the facility concerning my clothes, Momma checked me out against my doctor's orders. The staff at the facility was getting on to me for having a shirt that was showing my stomach, but I didn't have anything else to put on because they hadn't gone through my clothes yet. In an institution like that, they check all of your belongings for drugs or dangerous items before you can have them. My mom had brought me some clothes the last time she was there, but they never gave them to me. When Momma came back, after they got on to me about my shirt, she saw the clothes she had brought me, still in the same bag in the same place she had left them. That's when she signed me out of the hospital against doctor's orders.

When I got back home, I was put on homebound school. It took me a while to get back to myself after that breakdown. I had a really hard time adjusting. I never quit partying, but I did slow down a whole lot for a short period of time. The breakdown had really scared me. I was afraid, and deep down, even as a teenager, I think I knew that some of my problems were drug-related, but I didn't know how to stop or even if I could stop. The drug world was the only life I knew. Eventually, I went back to that world at full force.

Chapter Eleven

Long History of Abuse

I'm going to back up here and share a little bit about how abuse plagued my life from an early age. When I was very young, my parents were mentally, emotionally, verbally, and physically abusive toward each other. Neither of them was abusive toward me in any way when they were married. In fact, my dad never abused me (although it would be fair to say that his long-term neglect of our relationship left its own scars). My mom, on the other hand, was a different story. Momma always seemed to have abuse of some kind in her life. After my parents' divorce, Momma found her way into a string of abusive relationships with various boyfriends.

After suffering at the hands of others for most of her life, Momma started losing her temper and becoming abusive with *me*, beginning when I was around ten years old. I made excuses for her behavior, thinking that her actions were my fault. I was a mouthy kid, and, as I got older, it got worse. I was very disrespectful and completely unruly. She couldn't do anything with me, and I often provoked altercations with her. However, I now understand that my own behavior, as far from perfect as it was, was not an excuse for Momma physically abusing me. She was supposed to be the adult in the situation, not me. She was supposed to be in control. Although her outbursts rarely left bruises, it was nothing for her to slap my face or pop me in the mouth when I back-talked. She also thought it was okay to hit me with shoes, coat hangers, or whatever else she could get her hands on when she was mad.

It was really hard growing up like that, to be honest. In a way, it became normal, and, in another way, it was anything but normal. It was normal because that's all I knew; that's all I saw, and that's how I lived. It was anything but normal because it was embarrassing to have friends around when Momma would go off and start throwing fits, hitting me, cussing me, and yelling at me. Most of my friends from childhood quit coming around me in my teens because of my wild lifestyle. The few good friends that I did have left eventually started staying away because of my mom and the way she would lose her temper with me. There was only one who really stuck around through it all, and that was Lori. She loved my mom and knew she was a great person when she was in the right state of mind, but even Lori was afraid of Momma when she would flip out and start hitting me.

I tried to talk to my mom and tell her that the reason she lost it so badly on me was because of the way she had been abused by my grandmother. Even though there was a lot of truth in what I said, Momma refused to accept it. She believed that what she did to me was no comparison to what Nanny had done to her. This was true insomuch as I didn't have visible bruises for others to see at school, nor did I have to be taken out of the home by social services like Momma had been. Still, I did have many emotional scars. My bruises were on the inside, where no one could see them. I had inward marks that I carried around with me on a daily basis, caused from thinking that there must have been something terribly wrong with me to have one parent who was no longer involved in my life and another who chose to scream at me or beat me every time she got upset.

In time, I, too, became abusive when I got upset. I really didn't know any better, but I'm not making excuses for myself. This is just reality. It's all I knew. It's all I had seen. It's how I was raised. I didn't know what else to do with my anger. From that childhood incident with my toy monkey onward, I thought that's what you did when you got upset or mad: you hit, screamed, cussed, yelled, and threw stuff. No one had ever told me or shown me any different.

There's one particular incident that's very difficult for me to talk about, even all these years later. However, it is an important part of my story, so I need to share it with you. I was about fifteen, and the memory of that day is still very vivid in my mind, although I wish I could forget all about it. To some, it may not seem like a big deal; to others, it may seem like a huge thing. For me personally, it represents a crucial turning point in my life. Looking back, it was the moment when things really began to turn for the worse for me. I realize that looking at all that had already happened before that day, it is saying an awful lot to say that things were about to get even worse, but it's the truth. Something inside of me changed that day. My relationship with Momma shifted that day, as well, and I'm not sure that it was ever fully repaired. You might say that the metaphorical dog had been bitten one time too many and began biting back.

On that warm summer day, we had been out on our porch in the housing projects, shampooing our couch. Momma had rented a carpet shampooer to clean our furniture. Everything was going okay with the cleaning until Momma told me to go put some shoes on as it began to cool off that evening. I refused, telling her that I didn't need shoes, and it just went from there.

The memory of that afternoon is still so clear in my mind that I can remember exactly what I was wearing: a plain, pocket t-shirt with a pair of blue jean shorts. When I refused to go inside and put on a pair of shoes, Momma started coming at me, and I ran. I hurried inside the apartment and raced down the hallway to my bedroom. She followed me, got one of my shoes, and started beating me with it. Then, she pushed me down on my bed, got on top of me, straddled me with her knees on top of my arms so I couldn't hit back, and started beating me in my chest and stomach with her fists. Finally, I was able to get my feet and legs under her to kick her off of me. When I did, she landed hard on the hard tile floor and hit her head.

She was in shock that I had hurt her, and so was I. Although her physical abuse of me had been going on for several years at that point, I had never tried to defend myself before. I had run away from her, but I had never put up a fight. That time, I had nowhere to run.

I felt awful for hurting her. I couldn't believe I had hurt my momma. The guilt quickly set in. I felt like it was my fault for pushing her to that point over a stupid pair of shoes. It scared me to think I could really hurt someone I loved as much as I loved my mother, but it had happened. Momma blamed me, and I blamed her, but deep down, I put most of the responsibility for what had happened on myself.

You see, Momma wasn't always like that. She was actually a really sweet, loving person most of the time. Almost everybody loved Momma. Most of my newer friends called her Momma Becky. Of course, most of them never knew this side of Momma, this other person she became when she snapped. I don't know that I ever really knew that person either. I had some encounters with that person that were very unpleasant, but that wasn't really my momma, not deep down. Momma was a great person with a great heart. She just had a lot of problems from past abuse, drug abuse, and mental illness. I'm sure that it sounds like I am making excuses for her, but I feel that I need to explain her situation so that you will know that she wasn't a monster. I am not demonizing her. I loved her more than she may have ever known. She was just sick, very sick at times, and really needed healing. In later years, I would have to accept this fact myself so I could learn to love, forgive, and let go of the anger and animosity that I was holding towards both my mother and myself.

Before I reached that point, however, I would turn into a different person myself. Due to the abuse from Momma and other issues in my life, over time, I became abusive, too. First, I was abusive with Momma. Then, I became abusive toward my friends and boyfriends.

There were several times I argued with my friends, especially Lori, Leanne, and Kayla. I physically fought Kayla several times. They were pretty much knock-down-drag-outs, as they call them. I punched Leanne in the face one time while she was driving because we were arguing, but Lori and I never physically fought. We came close several times, but it never actually came to blows. To be honest, she was the first person in my life who ever really showed me love, true love, and what self-control was. During our biggest and worst argument ever, she used an amazing level of restraint.

We were at school, arguing. I don't remember what it was even about, so I'm sure it was probably something stupid. We were on a break in between classes, so the halls were full. While we were arguing, I took everything Lori was holding, books and all, and threw it down the hall in front of everybody. She got really mad and balled up her fist, but instead of hitting me, she walked away and went to the bathroom to get away from me. I followed her, continuing on with my ranting and raving for a few minutes, but then I stopped. I had never seen anyone pushed as far as I had pushed her and then have that person just walk away. I didn't know how to handle it. I think I was kind of in shock.

I had never seen anyone pushed to that point not fight back or at least continue to argue. She was done. She wasn't going to argue or fight with me anymore because she loved me. I know now that God was really using her to set an example for me. It was a representation of something that I had never seen before—an example of love, true love, not dysfunctional love. I still love Lori dearly and am very thankful for her and what she did for me that day. I never treated her like that again, but my anger and abuse problems didn't stop by any means. They just continued to get worse in other ways, including legal trouble.

The first time I ever really got in any trouble at school and with the police was for fighting. One day at school, when I was about sixteen, I decided to start arguing and fighting with this girl named Carrie. She had never really done anything to me, and I didn't really even know her very well. I just had a lot of anger issues and was looking for a reason to take it out on somebody—anybody. I see how childish, immature, and stupid it was now, but I didn't see it back then. I was too messed up to even consider how my actions affected others, and I thought it was cool to fight and basically bully people. Bullying was not talked about in school back then like it is now, but I can see that a bully is exactly what I was. I didn't go around calling people names and do that kind of bullying, but I did start a lot of fights, just like with Carrie. This one, however, took a turn that I didn't see coming.

I never really liked Carrie because she had kind of a snotty attitude. So, one day, she accidentally ran into me in the hallway at school. Even though it was an accident, I had found my chance and my excuse to fight her, so I shoved her into her locker. She didn't say a word. She just walked away. That infuriated me. I could not stand for someone to walk away from me. It wasn't like when Lori walked away because she loved me and didn't want to hurt me. This was totally different. I felt that this girl had disrespected me by ignoring my anger and walking off like she did. I wanted to fight! I wanted a reason to lay into her, and her walking away wasn't helping my rage at all. So, when she walked downstairs to her class, I followed her and flipped her desk over (She was not yet seated at the desk). I got sent to the assistant principal's office, and he gave me detention.

Well, it just so happened that I ended up in detention with her little brother, of all people. So, here was another chance for me to show myself and misbehave. That evening, when my ride came, Carrie came to pick up her little brother from detention. I tried to fight her in the parking lot like an idiot, but she would not get out of the car. When she left, I had my ride follow her. She even motioned for us to follow her, so we drove behind her all the way to her house. I jumped out of the car, and she acted like she wanted to fight—that is, until her mother came running out of the house screaming, "She's pregnant!" I apologized to her mom, told her I had no idea that Carrie was pregnant, and explained to her mother that she had motioned for us to follow her. We left after that, without it ever getting physical between Carrie and me.

I had some serious issues, but I wasn't yet so far gone that I was willing to fight someone who was expecting a baby. I did have some morals left, and I didn't ever want to hurt an innocent, unborn baby. Even though the fight stopped short of blows, Carrie and her mother pressed criminal charges. Linda, the driver, and I were also charged with criminal trespassing and assault with a deadly weapon for following her in the car.

Because it was our first encounter with the law, Linda and I both received pre-trial diversion. Linda received unsupervised probation, meaning that she basically just had to stay out of trouble, and the charges would be dismissed after a certain time. My own probation had to be supervised, however, because I failed the drug test that they gave us when we were working out the deal. We both had taken something to flush our systems, but mine didn't work as well hers because they found a trace of marijuana in mine. Or, maybe I just had more drugs in my system than she did; either way, the outcome was the same. I would be subjected to periodic visits with a probation officer, as well as random drug tests; if I messed up, I risked being sent away to juvenile detention.

Chapter Twelve

Battered and Bruised

Again, I need to back up a bit and explain the history of my abusive behavior. I didn't just erupt one day when I was in my mid-teens. I had actually been engaging in abusive behavior for quite some time, beginning when I was around twelve and in a relationship with Josh, my first serious, long-term boyfriend. If he didn't do exactly what I wanted or didn't give me what I wanted, I would cuss him and throw fits on him. The argument would usually lead to me slapping him, and sometimes I even punched him. Lori used to get so mad at me for being mean to him. He never really did anything in retaliation except to try to get away from me. He might have cussed me a little and called me crazy because of the way I acted, but he never laid a hand on me.

Then, I became involved with Michael. We dated off and on from my freshman year until my senior year of high school. This time, the roles were reversed. He was the abuser in the relationship most of the time, but I loved him. I was crazy about him. I thought that what we had was love because, in my mind, "love" meant a crazy, dysfunctional relationship with lots of abuse. Michael also came from an abusive background, just like me. As far as I know, nobody actually abused him, but he watched his dad, and one of his stepdads beat his mom for years. It's no wonder that our relationship was as messed up as it was; neither of us had any appropriate role models for teaching us how a healthy relationship was supposed to work.

The year that we got together, I was a freshman, and he was a senior. He was the star pitcher of the baseball team, and I thought he was great. To an outsider, we probably seemed like the perfect, all-American couple. His nickname was "Wonder" because he looked like a character from the television show *The Wonder Years*, except he had dark blonde hair and green eyes. When we started dating, people started calling me "Winnie" because, like the character by that name in the show, I had long dark hair and dark eyes.

Our first year together was pretty good, but after Michael graduated, things completely changed. He became extremely jealous. He was so jealous and controlling it became scary. In my mind, he had no reason to be jealous. I had always been a bit flirtatious and maybe a little too friendly toward other guys at times, but I never acted on it. He knew how I was when we got together, but once he graduated and wasn't at school to watch me, things started getting bad.

He would get messed up and start calling me names. I couldn't stand it when he did that. I would have rather been hit than called names, especially the names he called me. Maybe it was because I blamed myself for the rape and because I had been promiscuous at a young age. Despite those thoughts, I knew I wasn't what he was calling me. I had by no means been perfect, but I was not the horrible things he would say to me, not at that age anyway. I had always been faithful to any guy I had ever been with. I was a one-man kind of gal. I didn't like to be cheated on, so I didn't cheat on others. I just felt it was wrong and didn't like it. So, for me, the words he spoke hurt worse than anything he ever did to me physically. Physical wounds heal in time, but emotional and mental wounds don't go away so easily. The words play over and over in your mind, like seeds that sprout up, come into bloom, and change the way you think about yourself.

When I would get tired of him cussing me, I would hit him to get him to hit me back, so he would shut up. Crazy as it sounds, this tactic was fairly effective in ending a fight. Michael would feel bad for hitting me, apologize, and promise he would never hurt me again. He would tell me that he loved me and that he would do better. I wanted to believe it, and maybe on the surface, I did, but, deep down, I knew better.

I can kind of understand why battered wives stay with their husbands. They make you believe it's your fault and that if you would act right, then they wouldn't have to beat you. They make you think that you're worthless and that no one else would want you. You think you can't survive without them, that you really love them, and that if you could just love them enough, they would change. You think they really love you, but what an abusive man feels for a woman is not really love. Love doesn't hurt like that. God is love. Abuse is not of God.

The first time any of my family, other than Momma, witnessed the abuse between Michael and me was at Nanny's house. My friend Molly brought me home from school one day. Michael's mom lived across the road from Nanny, so he was watching for me, as usual. If he wasn't sitting at the park next to the school waiting for me, then he would be waiting for me at home. I was ten minutes later than what he expected, and he flipped out. Molly dropped me off in the driveway, and here he came across the road.

He followed me into Nanny's house, questioning me about why I was late. Momma and Aunt Sissy were in the kitchen, but Nanny had gone somewhere that day. So, Michael and I were alone in the living room. I was trying to get him away from Momma and Aunt Sissy because I knew things were about to get bad, really bad. They could still hear everything going on between us, but they couldn't see us. I had turned my back to him and started walking toward Nanny's recliner when he popped me right in the back of the head. He actually thumped me, with his fist, right in the back of my head. I went down face first on those old hardwood floors.

You have to remember, I was just a teenager, maybe sixteen years old, seventeen at the most. I might have weighed 115-125 pounds back then. He was a few years older and had been an athlete—the star pitcher on the high school baseball team—so when he hit, it wasn't some little punch. He would really hit me and really hit hard, but that time at Nanny's was the first time he had ever knocked me down like that. It was also the first time he had done something like that around my family. He was normally able to keep better control of his temper when we were around other people.

Up until then, Michael's physical abuse had been limited to times when we were alone and/or when he was really drunk, but he wasn't drunk that day at all. Also, he tended to hit me on the head rather than in the face where his fist would leave marks. This shows that he had some control over his actions and that he knew what he was doing. Mostly, he hit where no one could see the marks; I had pump knots on my head from being beaten by him. One time, his battering got so bad that I literally tried to jump out of the car we were riding in. We were stopped at a stop sign in the middle of town in his mother's old blue Malibu. He was hitting me hard, and I desperately wanted to get away from him. I opened my passenger door and tried to jump out of the car, but he grabbed me by the hair of my head, my ponytail to be exact, and wouldn't let go. Knowing I was defeated, I just closed the door and took it. I knew there was no getting away.

That day when he hit me in the back of the head at my Nanny's house, it wasn't any more painful than all the blows that he had inflicted on me in the past. Sadly, I was kind of used to it by then. It did hurt me in another way, though. He had taken something shameful that had been just between the two of us and exposed it to my family. Momma and Aunt Sissy responded to him beating me by telling him that the best thing that he could do was to get out of the house. Considering their own pasts, it's a wonder they didn't flog him right there, but neither of them did, not that day anyway. I guess they were just so used to seeing men hit women that it didn't seem all that out of the ordinary to them at the time for a teenage girl to get beat up by her boyfriend right there in the living room.

The worst beating that I ever got from Michael happened after a party at a friend's house. Michael got drunk and became insanely jealous of everybody. We had to leave the party because of the way he was acting. He was completely out of control. He was always scary on liquor, but that night he was drinking Wild Turkey, and it made *him* a wild turkey. He would hit me, apologize, and then start again—in front of everybody at the party. It's like he couldn't quit. He couldn't control himself. I had never seen him like that before. It was like something had taken him over.

I took him to my mom's apartment because I didn't want him to go home like that. I didn't want his mom to see him in that kind of shape. I was hoping he could sober up some before he went home, but it didn't work out that way. It was just a repeat of what had been happening at the party, except there wasn't much apologizing or stopping once he no longer had an audience. He was so messed up and so mean that I was afraid of what might happen. I decided that the best thing to do would be to get him to go home. Again, it didn't quite work out that way. We ended up outside fighting, in the middle of the night, in the parking lot between Momma's apartment and his mom's house.

While I was in the parking lot trying to help him get back to his mother's place, he picked me up and head-butted me. I hit the ground. The blow stunned me. I had never been hit that hard before in my life! When I was finally able to get back up, we continued on to his mother's house. His mom and I were able to get him inside the house briefly, but he kept trying to get back out the door so that he could get closer to me and continue the beating. During this time, he closed his mom's finger in the screen door. She ended up having to go to the hospital and get stitches that night, but I got away. She yelled for me to run, and I did.

Immediately, I had a big knot come up on my head. It turned all different colors, and Momma was worried that I had a concussion. She begged me to go to the hospital, but I refused. I knew they would ask me what happened and that the authorities would try to make me press charges against Michael. I had no intention of doing that. Even if I said I didn't want Michael to be prosecuted criminally, I knew there was a chance that the State might move forward anyway (After all, I was still a minor.) This sounds so crazy in hindsight to forgo medical treatment in order to protect the person who had hurt me. I must have thought I deserved to be mistreated. After all, I had also protected my rapist by not reporting what had happened, and I had also excused my mother's terrible behavior in front of my friends.

My relationship with Michael never got any better; instead, it just got worse. There was another time when we were outside fighting in his mom's yard during the middle of the day, and he wouldn't let me go. I was trying to go back to Momma's apartment, but I couldn't break free from him. Momma and her boyfriend pulled up to the apartment and saw what was going on. They told him to stop it, but he kept right on hitting me. Momma walked into his mother's house, got one of his mom's skillets, came back outside, and started beating Michael with it. Needless to say, he let go of me then, and the fight stopped. His mom wasn't home that day, but even if she had been, I don't think she would have said anything to Momma about Momma hitting him with the skillet. Michael's mom always tried to take up for me and to protect me, but it didn't work out so well sometimes.

Our last fight was on a night when we were out drinking with his cousin and his cousin's wife. When we started arguing, they took us to Nanny's. We were in the kitchen, and Nanny was in the living room. She could hear us but couldn't see us. He said something to me, I pushed him, and he hit the floor. He was drunk, and his shoes were wet, or I could have never pushed him down like that. He was a lot bigger and stronger than me. He hit the floor pretty hard, and then he started cussing me, saying, "You _____ _____, I ought to _____ kill you!" Nanny heard what Michael said and called the police.

I tried to get him over to his mom's house before the police got there, but we were in the middle of the road arguing when the cop pulled up. Michael was drunk, but the officer gave him a break and didn't take him to jail. I told the officer that Michael hadn't hit me but admitted that I had hit him. It was true; I had hit him and pushed him, trying to get him to shut up and go home. Neither of us wanted to press charges, so the police officer let both of us go that night. However, he contacted the District Attorney's office about Michael, and domestic violence charges were filed against him a few days later. We went to court, and I asked for the charges to be dropped. The judge issued a mutual restraining order, stating that neither of us was to be within one hundred yards of the other.

Soon after that, we finally split up for good. We were friendly and even partied together a few times after the restraining order ended, but our relationship finally came to an end about halfway through my senior year.

Chapter Thirteen

My Senior Year

This chapter will back up to the beginning of my senior year, before Michael and I split up. My senior year was one of the worst years of my life. I really don't even like to think about it, and I definitely don't like to talk about it. It brings up a lot of strong emotions. Your senior year is supposed to be one of the most important and memorable years of your life, not one of the lowest points in your life like mine was.

At the beginning of the year, it seemed as if things were looking up. Momma got a promotion at her job. She was still working for Plateau Mental Health Center, and they were awarded funding to start a Drop-In-Center, a place where those suffering from mental illness could relax and enjoy the company of others dealing with similar issues. Momma was chosen to get the center up and running, as well as to manage the center once it was open. This gave her the opportunity to not only create the entire program but also to run it as she saw fit, within certain guidelines. This was a huge deal for her and for us. Things were looking up for our little family! This was also a huge step up for Momma in her current line of work.

She was able to find a beautiful older home at a great location near Tennessee Tech in Cookeville, Tennessee. The center had an exercise room, a craft room, a media room, and a kitchen area. There was also a cozy little area set up outside for members to relax and enjoy the sunshine. Momma did an exceptional job. The center was really nice, and the clients loved it.

Momma's salary was increased to $1,500 a month. I know that may not seem like much to some people, but this was in the late 1990s. At the time, it was really good money for us. We were still receiving child support, also. Everything seemed to finally be turning our way, but the moment was fleeting. Momma had been given too much power and too much money for someone who struggled with addiction.

For a while there, Momma had managed to keep her addiction under control fairly well. Although she dabbled in the harder stuff like cocaine and crank a few times before my senior year, she was not a regular user like I was. She sold pot and a little cocaine a few times to cover the expenses of our drug use, but she never had a habit to where it controlled her instead of her controlling it. That was all soon to end. She had found her match, her drug of choice—crack—cocaine.

Momma started dating a guy named Billy from Cookeville. He was already a heavy user of crack. I really didn't know the extent of what was going on. I was in Monterey with Michael most of the time while she was out with Billy in Cookeville. I thought she was just busy with work and her new boyfriend. We did all smoke crack together a few times, and I went with Momma and Billy to his place several times to party, but I still didn't understand that she was getting hooked. I had never seen her truly hooked on anything, and she was keeping it hidden from me pretty well.

The night that Momma and I went to Algood Manor Apartments, I knew something was up. Somehow, I knew something was different, that something had changed in my momma. She wasn't really *my momma* anymore. She was somebody totally different. I had never seen her like that before, and I wish that I had never seen her like that period, to be very honest. The feeling I got at this place was awful. It was almost like something came on me and covered me and was lingering all around me, from the time I got there until the time I left. It was very dark and eerie.

Algood was a small town located about fifteen miles from Monterey. At the time, it was known as "crack central." The saying around town within the partying crowd was, "It's all good in Algood." I beg to differ. It was anything but good where I was that night with Momma. The community itself was not bad, but where we were on that particular evening, things were bad. Really, really bad. People were walking around slinging dope (selling drugs), especially crack, and turning tricks (prostituting themselves) to get high. It was awful. It was like something you see on television about the worst of the worst in an inner-city, certainly not something you would expect to see on the streets of a small Southern town.

Momma got strung out really bad on crack very quickly. It didn't take long for her to lose her job and, essentially, to leave me. She was in really bad shape. This was the first time my mom had truly abandoned me for drugs. I rarely saw her. I lived on my child support checks if I managed to get to the mailbox before she did.

I stayed so messed up on pills and weed that I really didn't care about what Momma was doing, or at least that was what I told myself. In truth, I just tried to stay numb to the hurt that I was feeling. Until then, my mom had always put me first. She loved me and had always made sure my needs were met, even before her own needs, and now I felt l like I didn't even have a mom. The mother that I knew and loved was no longer there. Even when I saw her physical body, Momma wasn't there. She was gone.

Even through all the mental illness, suicide attempts, and abuse, I had never seen my mom like this. There were times when she had momentary lapses where she wasn't herself due to mental illness or losing her temper, but she would come back to herself fairly fast. This time she was gone, really gone, and I didn't know where she was or how to find her. She was just a shell of a person. My momma wasn't there anymore. It didn't take long before we lost everything.

One recovery program says that "jails, institutions, and death" are the inevitable end for someone struggling with addiction unless they surrender their life to God and get the help they need. Momma's path through addiction included jail. She had written several bad checks, and a warrant was issued for her arrest.

Momma, Billy, and I were at the apartment. I guess she had run out of money, dope, and checks by then. A county deputy came by, picked her up, and took her to jail. I was hysterical. I completely lost it when he took my momma to jail. No matter what she had done, I still loved her. I got mad and upset, absolutely furious with her at times, but I never once stopped loving her. She was my momma. She was my world. No matter how dysfunctional our relationship was, it was all we knew, and all we had was each other.

After she was booked at the county jail, no one would help me get her out. Now, I know she was actually being helped instead of being hurt because she was not being enabled to continue living the kind of lifestyle she had been living as long as she was behind bars. However, at the time, I was hurt, disappointed, and angry that my family was not there for me or my mom. I guess I expected them to help her or at least help me, but they didn't. In my mind, it was as if they had decided that I was grown and could take care of myself and everything else without their help, but that wasn't true at all. I was just seventeen years old and was left to figure it all out on my own.

The day Momma appeared in court, I had to go to the courthouse all by myself. No one even offered to go with me—not my grandmother, not my uncle, not my aunt. No one. I could perhaps have understood if my mom had been in a lot of legal trouble over the years, and this was the "last straw," but this was the first time she had ever been arrested. She had never been in any kind of trouble with the court system before, whereas Uncle Nick and Aunt Sissy had been in trouble multiple times. Momma was usually the one there with Nanny to bail them out, but this didn't happen in Momma's case. No one attempted to help Momma in any way. I had to watch my mom come into the courtroom in a blue, jail-issued jumpsuit with shackles around her wrists and ankles without anyone there to help me or even to be moral support. It was the most alone I had ever felt up to that point in my life.

That image of Momma coming into the courtroom is something I wish I had never seen, a mental picture I wish I could completely erase from my memory. No child should ever have to see their parent in that kind of situation. I know my momma had done the crime, and it was up to her to do the time, and I was by no means innocent myself, but when you see your parent, the only parent that had really been that constant in your life, standing there as a completely broken person in shackles and chains it really does something to you. I can't really even begin to explain the feelings of shock, hurt, and embarrassment that I had. The feeling of anger that I have even now, just thinking back on it, is hard to put into words. There was so much anger—toward my family, their choices, my own choices, addiction, drugs, and what they did to me and my family, etc.

I love my family, and I have chosen to forgive them, but it doesn't make these feelings go away when I think about the details all over again. I don't have any anger toward the court system or police in any way. They were doing their job and, in a sense, trying to save our lives, but we were doing the exact opposite. We were slowly killing ourselves. I think deep down, my greatest anger is from wondering why no one would even try to help us. Why couldn't anyone see that we were killing ourselves? If they did see it, why didn't they try to do anything about it? Why did they just let it go on and on and not try to intervene in any way? I guess the true answer is that they couldn't. Nanny and the rest of our family had plenty of troubles of their own, and they had very few resources to spare. Even if they had tried to help us, I'm not sure that anyone could have done much to truly help us get off of the path that we were on.

That day in court, the judge set Momma's bail for $500. I had $43 dollars left to my name from my latest child support check. I called a bail bonding company from the jail. A sweet little lady from the agency showed up. She needed 10 percent of the bond in cash to bond Momma out. She gave me the $7 I needed to make the 10 percent. God had to have sent that lady to me that day. I don't know of any bonding companies who are willing to give you money like that woman did. I'm sure she felt sorry for me, a seventeen-year-old girl all alone, trying to bail her mother out of the county jail.

I was so happy to see my momma when she was finally released. It was such a relief to see her without shackles and in street clothes. I was glad to finally be able to touch her and hug her, but she was in horrible shape mentally and emotionally. Her nerves were absolutely shot. She had paced the floors until she had worn blisters on the bottoms of her feet. I'm sure some of it was caused by drug use and withdrawals, but I believe it was also caused by fear. Momma always had a fear of incarceration, both for herself and for anyone in the family, because of the way that my grandfather had died in jail. Unfortunately, not even the fear of going back to jail was enough to stop Momma. We went straight to Billy's house from the jail so that Momma could get high. She stayed there with Billy, and I went back home to Michael.

It got worse before it got better. I lived alone in our apartment for a while without a phone, cable, electricity, or water. Michael's mom made sure I ate and showered at their house, and my uncle Nick carried a five-gallon bucket of water across the road from Nanny's to flush the commode daily—until, finally, we lost the apartment completely. I came home from school one day to find that the locks had been changed on the front door. I called the landlord. I was a hysterical mess and threw a fit. I acted terribly, but I didn't know what else to do. The landlord was very nice, all things considered. He couldn't let me stay in the apartment, but he did send one of his workers to let me go inside to get my clothes so I could at least go to school the next day.

I was so angry and scared. I was still just a kid, and I had no home, no food, no money, and, for all intents and purposes, no mother. I didn't know what to do. I kept it all hidden from my dad and stepmom, who lived in another state at that time. I also kept it hidden from most of my friends at school and their parents.

Eventually, my mom and I moved back in with Nanny. By this time, we had lost everything again, including our car. All of our belongings, including most of my baby pictures and several other sentimental items, were put into a storage building. In time, we lost all of that stuff, too. It would be years before I would feel the full effects of the loss of the memorabilia of my childhood.

At the end of my senior year, right after I turned eighteen and after Michael and I split up, I got into some more trouble myself. I had taken a bunch of Momma's Xanax, her nerve pills, before heading to Cookeville to hang out with my friend, Molly. I was already pretty messed up on the nerve pills when I decided to go into Kroger and, like an idiot, steal some Zimas (an alcoholic beverage). I went out to the car, drank the Zimas, and then went back into the store for more. That's when I got busted, the second time that I went in. I'm sure they saw me the first time because I was anything but sly about it. I was maybe 110 pounds by then, and that was pushing it. I had lost weight from using and partying, and I was hiding the bottles of alcohol in my shorts. I was wearing my little cut-off jean short-shorts, and I had on a tiny tank belly shirt. So, I know they had to see them the first time, but I guess by the second time, they had to do something with me. Some of the employees took me into the office until the cops got there to charge me with shoplifting and arrest me.

When Molly saw the cops arrive and I still hadn't come out of the store, she figured out what had happened and came into the store. She begged the cops not to take me to jail. She told them that she had no way to get ahold of my mom but that if they let her, she would take me straight home. They wrote a citation for theft under $500, illegal consumption by possession, and public intoxication. Then, they let me go.

I don't remember getting into any trouble with Momma about the incident at Kroger. I assume Momma felt that she had no right to punish me after all she had done. That was the first time I had gotten in trouble as an adult, so they only gave me probation and fines. I would also now have a permanent criminal record—not exactly a bright start to adulthood.

Despite that little blip on my radar, I did not stop drinking, using drugs, or partying in general. Momma did stop smoking pot and doing crack for a while; because of the bad check conviction, she was on probation and had to start taking monthly drug tests. All I remember her taking for a while there was her prescription medication. Her whole ordeal must have scared her, but mine didn't faze me. I never even slowed down. I actually went into overdrive and started using crystal meth more during this time.

My mom bought me stuff every month from the head shop (a place where you can get pipes, bongs, and other things related to drug use) so that I could pass the drug tests that I was required to take as a condition of my probation. I could tell that Momma was really scared about the possibility of me going to jail, but I was not. For so long, she had bailed me out whenever I had gotten into a tight spot and had taken care of things, so I didn't have a normal, rational fear of jail or getting into trouble. She, on the other hand, had a very real and understandable fear of jail because of what had happened to my grandfather, Oden.

Chapter Fourteen

The Needle

In spite of all the craziness in my life up to that point, I somehow managed to graduate from high school in May 1999. Once I graduated, there was nothing anchoring me anymore. Even though I had missed quite a bit of school because of my drug issues, all of the things going on with my mother, and my general state of near-homelessness during my senior year, school had still grounded me to some extent. Yes, I partied and "did my thing," but I still knew that I had to go to school. Otherwise, I would get in trouble for truancy. Momma would get in trouble, too, and I definitely did not want that to happen.

After graduation, things went downhill fast. With nothing holding me back anymore, I started using crystal meth daily. I had used meth on a fairly regular basis during my senior year, but I was still able to take it or leave it at that point. I really liked it—and I loved the high that I got from it—but I was not yet to the point where *it* controlled *me*. Honestly, there wasn't any drug that truly controlled my life at that time. Yes, I had an addiction. I used drugs daily, and I had for years. I always smoked pot and did whatever else was around, but there was not that one drug that really had control of me like the Valium and crack had back when I was younger. That all changed in the summer of 1999.

During that summer, I started eating, snorting, and/or smoking crystal meth every day. It immediately became my drug of choice. I wanted it above any and every other drug. I would leave cocaine, pot, or pills laying for meth. I began to fall in love with meth in a way that I had never experienced before, and an incredibly powerful addiction set in. The more meth I used, the more I wanted. No matter how much I got or how much I used, however, I could never get enough. This is when I really started to lose myself, when I truly entered the meth world. I had been a drug addict for years, but the world of meth was something totally different.

I'm not minimizing the drug world or maximizing the meth world, but I have lived in both, and I can tell you that there is definitely a difference between the two. At one time or another, I have been hooked on a little bit of everything except heroin, and that was only because there wasn't much heroin around in the area in which I grew up (at least at that time), and nothing compares to the world of meth—nothing. I am not saying that it is necessarily more addictive per se, although there have been some studies to suggest that it could be. Like many other illegal substances, meth is extremely addictive, but what I'm talking about is the way that it makes you act, think, and feel. It changes you as a person.

Becoming a meth addict is like entering the twilight zone. It causes you to become paranoid and to hallucinate. Crystal meth has the power to make you hear and see things that are not real, are not there, and do not exist; however, to the person tripping (hallucinating), these things are very real, if not more real, than reality itself. I think this was why meth became the ultimate high for me because I could truly escape from reality. All the stress, the pain, and the hurt were no longer there. I could go to a faraway place where no one could find me and where I honestly could not find myself, and that is exactly what I wanted to do: lose myself, escape from reality, and forget about my life and everything about life in general.

When I was taking meth, I would stay up for days, even weeks, to the point that I would lose count of how many days I had been up and how long it had been since I had eaten. The meth completely changed me. I had always been ambitious and had goals in life, but it got to where my only goal was to get high. I had wanted to get high and stay high for years, but I still had morals, plans, and dreams. This part of me was slowly fading away, and things would only continue to get worse. Part of me knew something was dying and that I was changing, and at times it was scary. Still, my desire and love for the drug overpowered any fear that I had. Soon, my desire for drugs grew much stronger than any desire I had ever had for a better future or for the dreams I once held so dear to my heart.

When I was young, I said I wanted to be the first woman President of the United States of America. This dream soon faded when I decided I wanted to be a veterinarian. This one lasted until I was in high school. During high school, I began to think about becoming a school teacher, but I wanted to specifically work in special education due to a job my mom had working with individuals with intellectual disabilities when I was younger and we lived in McMinnville. I loved her clients and thought they were so precious. This would soon be my major when I began community college at Roane State Community College in Crossville, Tennessee.

Most of my "using buddies" had already been hooked on meth for a while at that point. Finishing high school and having the desire to attend college kept me on track for a little bit compared to others I was around, but it wasn't enough. My buddies were all older than me and lived a life totally consumed by addiction. They didn't go to school or college, and they didn't work. Once they had started shooting up (using drugs intravenously), the quest for meth and the high that came with it became their life.

Leanne (you may recall her as one of the others involved in the wreck where we lost our friend Stephen) and my so-called boyfriend, Luke, had started shooting up together. They tried to hide it from me and wouldn't do it around me, but I knew what was going on. They seemed to be so much higher than me. It didn't seem fair. I wanted to feel what they were feeling and be high like them, but they refused to let me try it. I believe they were already hooked pretty badly and knew that, if I ever tried it, I was sure to be a fiend who couldn't stop. I was already the type who asked for dope constantly, especially when I was smoking it. I could never get enough. I would drive everyone around me crazy asking for more.

Looking back, I can very easily see how addiction is progressive in nature. It has to do with the method in which the meth goes into the user's system. Most people who use drugs start out taking drugs by mouth, then snorting, then smoking, and then, when none of that will get them high enough anymore, they go to the needle. Not all people who do meth (or drugs in general) make it that far. Not all are willing to go that far, thank God, because the needle is a whole other addiction in and of itself.

I've heard lots of people in active addiction try to justify their using behavior. For example, if they just take drugs by mouth, then they say, "I don't have a problem because I'm not snorting." Then when they start snorting, they say, "I don't have a problem because I'm not smoking." Then when they start smoking, they say, "Well, at least I'm not sticking a needle in my arm like those 'junkies' over there." Then when they become the "junkie" over there sticking the needle in their arm, they have gone too far to care anymore.

As an eighteen-year-old, recent high school graduate, this is where I would soon find myself. I had never said the phrases I used above, but I had thought them to myself many times. In my mind, as long as I wasn't using the needle, I was somehow better than those who were injecting meth intravenously. For anyone who has never been in the drug world, there are "classes" or divisions that you need to understand. Different drugs and different means of using the drugs and different means to obtain the drugs are looked down upon within certain crowds. For example, to a causal drug user who is still at the recreational stage of just smoking pot and occasionally popping a few pills, those who use harder drugs, especially those who shoot up, are looked down upon. I had somewhat cared about that at one time, but that was all soon to change because, the very first time I ever shot up, I shot crystal meth, and I was hooked, severely hooked. I no longer cared about my status within the drug world or much of anything else for that matter.

My first time shooting meth was on a summer night in 1999, not long at all after graduation. I was out with Josh, my ex-boyfriend, and he introduced me to a girl named Arora. Her boyfriend and Josh cooked dope together (unlike most drugs that are sold on the street after coming into the country via an established supply chain, meth is made locally by "cooks"). We all went to Arora's boyfriend's apartment, a "meth house" in the housing projects in Cookeville. I talked Arora into letting me shoot up. Arora, some guy that had dope, and I all went into the bedroom. The guy knew I had never shot up before, so he fixed me up a big shot. It hit me, and that was the moment that I fell in love with crystal meth. From that point on, I just wanted more and more and more. I could never get enough. When that first shot hit me, I felt complete euphoria. I didn't care about anyone or anything else in this world. After that first experience, I just wanted to chase that high. As time went on, I would need more and more meth to recapture that same feeling.

Despite my past experience with a wide variety of drugs, it was that moment when I first felt meth coursing through my veins that truly changed my life. I had never felt like this about any drug before or any high before. I thought I was truly in love for the first time in my life, and I finally understood why none of my buddies would let me try it. By the time I figured it out, it was too late. I had finally done it, and I couldn't stop. I was hooked. I was completely and totally addicted to methamphetamine. I couldn't focus on anything but the drug and getting high and enjoying the high.

I no longer thought about whether I should go home or whether Momma would worry because she didn't know where I was. She got upset because I didn't call to check in and let her know I wasn't coming home. Before I started shooting up with meth, I normally checked in at least every other day or so to let her know I was alive, but now I was in another world. I didn't care about Momma, checking in, or anything else except getting higher. I didn't realize or care how dangerous it was or that it was about to destroy my life. All I cared about was getting high. I literally couldn't see or think about anything else. I was fully consumed.

After I shot up that first time, Josh was crushed. He knew what we were getting ready to do before we ever went into the bedroom. He kept looking at me, and I knew that look. He didn't want me to go in there because he knew that guy was getting ready to fix me up. We weren't a couple anymore and hadn't been for years, but he still cared about me and what happened to me. He was one of my best friends. We actually got along much better after we split up and quit dating. Josh was one of the very few good guys I knew who still had a good heart. He had a drug problem, yes, but the drugs hadn't completely turned him and hardened him like it had so many others I knew back in those days. He knew I had planned on going to college and doing something with my life, and I believe he knew at that very moment that I had just flushed all that down the toilet along with any morals I had left.

I did make somewhat of an effort to go to college for a couple of semesters, but it didn't last. I couldn't keep it up. The addiction had too great of a hold on me by this time. My childhood best friend, Lori, drove me back and forth to classes, or I wouldn't have ever made it as far as I did. I was in a definite downward spiral, and I was not looking up. Because of my addiction, Lori and I didn't really hang out together anymore and hadn't for a long time other than at school. She hadn't been using for quite some time, and she knew I was getting in bad shape. She really put herself out there and in harm's way by coming and getting me every day, but she wouldn't give up on me. Maybe she thought that if she could get me to school, something would change in my life. Maybe she was just trying to help me hang on. There were lots of times that she came to get me, and I couldn't even make it to school. It was always because I was either too high or not high enough. If I was too high, I was too geeked out, and if I wasn't high enough, I didn't have enough energy to get me there.

There were many days that she talked me into going when I really didn't need to be out in public because I had been up partying all night. I would go with good intentions of going to class. Sometimes I would even make it through a class or maybe two, but then I would have to go to the car and pass out because I didn't have any more dope to make it through the day. On the days I couldn't make it, Lori would push me to at least get my homework done so she could turn it in for me. She was working harder for me than I was. Obviously, she believed in me more than I believed in myself.

I do actually remember trying at times during all this. I didn't just completely sit down and give up. I was just too addicted to be able to overcome it, but I had not totally given myself over to it, not just yet. I remember sitting up using, all night, while doing homework, somehow thinking I was going to be able to get a college education despite the fact that I was now shooting meth on a regular basis. Needless to say, I didn't make it. I flunked out during my very first year of college.

After I flunked out, I continued going downhill fast. Once everyone knew I had tried the needle, most of my buddies let me do it with them, even if I was still a few years younger than most of them. I also began to move out of proverbial frying pan and closer to the fire. I wasn't just using meth anymore, I was getting involved with people who were into the cooking scene pretty hot and heavy. Leanne and I did a lot of running for the local cooks and dealers, which means that we went out to get the chemicals and supplies needed to cook the meth.

Back then, meth was made the old-fashioned way that took days to prepare and make. There were three main ingredients: white (pseudoephedrine), black (iodine crystals), and red (red phosphorous). Other items had to be bought like lye or Coleman Fuel and acetone, as well as the cooking utensils like Pyrex and tubing. The police had really been cracking down on all of these items. You could only buy so many bottles or packs of pills; later, they made you sign for them and then eventually made it almost impossible to get the ingredients to make meth. That's when the shake-and-bake method came about—this was after my time. The game was still in full play while I was in it. The authorities were just beginning to learn how to get a hold on the meth problem. The same was happening at the Farm Bureau to get iodine and at other places to buy large quantities of matches.

That's where we came in. This is how we were supplied with our dope for a while. As long as we did the running, then the cook didn't have to take a chance on getting busted running in and out of stores getting supplies, and hauling them around. We tried to do whatever was needed in order to protect the cook because that's how we were assured we had dope. We also helped prepare some of the chemicals and supplies, like scraping matches, making iodine crystals, and straining pills (separating the active ingredients in the pseudoephedrine from the inert part that would be thrown away).

The main cook that we started out helping, nicknamed Doc, had already been busted once and knew the cops were watching him, but we even cooked dope at the same house where the police had busted him before. We must have thought we were invincible or invisible; either way, we were not very smart (Spoiler alert: Doc eventually got busted again, was sent to the penitentiary, and died in prison from cirrhosis of the liver).

Back when we were running for Doc, Leanne and I still got out and partied a lot. We went to the bars dancing and partying. We would get high, then drink and dance all night. Despite all the chaos and insanity in my life, I thought I was still having fun at that point. After Doc went to prison, things started to change. Leanne started living with the biggest cook in town, David. He had a lot of people who helped him cook and sell, like Danny and Luke. Luke was the guy I was dating at the time. David used him and Danny to cook meth for him most of the time to protect himself. They were also known as two of the "best" and main cooks in the area.

Of course, Leanne and I always had plenty of dope because we were both dating cooks. This would have been in the summer of 2000, about a year after I graduated from high school when we became really strung out. We had been bad off for a while, but that summer, we went to a whole other level of strung out. We had become true "needle addicts." We had stopped going to the clubs and partying. We didn't get out and socialize unless it was absolutely necessary in order to get our fix. It wasn't fun anymore, but we had no plans of changing or getting out. We were hooked—hook, line, and sinker, and we were sinking fast.

We wore three-quarter length sleeved shirts, long-sleeved shirts, or jackets in the middle of the summer to cover up our track marks from shooting up. We had all kinds of hats and different colored sunglasses to match our clothes. We wore our hats pulled down to where they would just about meet our glasses. It's like we felt nobody could see us or notice our bugged-out eyes as long as we were all covered up. In reality, we were just drawing more attention to ourselves. We had lost so much weight and changed so much; it was sad. Our eyes were bugged out and sunk in all at the same time, with cheekbones beginning to sink in, and I would get sores on me from meth seeping out of my pores and from picking at my face.

This is when I really, truly started feeling bad about myself. I was ashamed and embarrassed at times. I was so paranoid that most days, I couldn't stand myself, but I didn't see any way out. To be honest, I'm not sure I really wanted out. I just know I was starting to become miserable, but I couldn't stop. I was getting to the point where I didn't really like to go out in public, and I didn't really like myself anymore. It's hard to think about how it really made me feel deep down, to know I was losing myself, to know I was shunned by my friends. Lots of them didn't even want to be around me or have anything to do with me anymore because I was so far out there. There's a big difference between being the life of the party and only living to party, which is where I was at that point: my only desire in life was to get high. "Party girls" and "needle-junkies" are two very different types of people, and I knew deep inside which one I had become. I don't use the term "needle-junkie" derogatory toward anyone who has used the needle to get high. This was the derogatory internal dialogue I used when thinking of myself. I felt awful about who I was, what I had become, and what I was doing.

There is one incident in particular that sticks out in my mind. There was a guy, Willy, who I had grown up with. He was like a brother to me, and we had been really close for years. He partied some, too, but didn't really do any hard drugs. After I got in really bad shape, he wouldn't even speak to me. I followed him all over the city park one day, just trying to get him to talk to me, but he wouldn't. He refused. I still remember the look on his face. I could see the disappointment and hurt in his eyes because I had become so strung out and had changed so much. It still hurts to think about what happened, but I understand it a little bit now. I wasn't the same person anymore. I didn't act the same, didn't look the same, and most definitely didn't think the same. I was gone. Spiritually, mentally, and emotionally, I had checked out.

Around this same time, I also came close to checking out physically, as in leaving this world for good. One night, I got together with Leanne's boyfriend, David. I did it because Leanne was out with (or had been out with) my boyfriend, Luke. It was revenge, just another part of how things rolled in the crazy drug world we were involved in back then.

David and I and another guy named Danny went to a friend's place out of town to finish up a big batch of dope. We left some with them for letting us cook at their place and took the rest with us to David's trailer. When we got there, Danny passed out on the couch because he had been up for too long. David and I went into the bathroom, where we always went for him to hit me (shoot me up). He fixed me up a big shot and hit me. I had never done one that big before. What he gave me was about the same amount that Leanne and I normally split, and he usually always gave her the first and biggest shot. As soon as it really hit me, I knew I had done too much, and I was scared. At that point, I had never done a shot that had scared me before, not like this, and you have to remember, I was barely nineteen years old at the time.

I made it to his bedroom, and I just laid there. I couldn't move. I started to shut my eyes, and he started saying my name and laughing. I don't know if he thought it was funny or what, but I didn't think it was funny at all. I was scared. I could feel my eyes twitching, which had never happened before. I had never done that much meth before (Methamphetamine is a stimulant, which is why my eyes were twitching). I felt like I was going to pass out, something you should not do on meth; as a stimulant, it should keep you awake, not cause you to pass out. This is when I knew I had done way too much. I managed to get up and stagger to the bathroom. When I looked in the mirror, I could literally see my eyeballs bobbing up and down. It was one of the freakiest things that I have ever seen in my life!

Moving around helped me a little, but I couldn't stay up, so I went back and laid down on the bed. By this time, I think he was getting kind of concerned and knew I had done too much, so he sat on the edge of the bed and kept me from going to sleep. In doing so, he probably saved my life. Of course, he was also the one who gave me the dope that almost killed me, but I did ask for it. To his credit, he stayed there with me and kept me awake until the effects of the dope wore off. If he hadn't, I think I would have gone to sleep and never woken up.

Chapter Fifteen

Rejection

As evidenced by my near-fatal overdose, my life had become a mess. It was an absolutely miserable state of existence. It got to the point where I was always paranoid and tripped on people all the time, thinking they were snitches and working for the police. Ironically, I even tripped on my uncle Nick (Yes, the same one that had come to Nanny's house early one morning when I was getting ready to go to school several years earlier, convinced that there were police officers in the trees surrounding our house). Logically, I knew that my uncle wasn't any kind of informant because he had done time over a meth lab that wasn't even his. He was pulled over, and the lab was in the trunk of his car. It didn't belong to him, but Uncle Nick refused to tell the truth—that it belonged to one of the other guys in the car—and, eventually, ended up spending about nine months in the county jail and was later sent to a halfway house.

You would think that would have been enough for me to realize that Uncle Nick wasn't a "snitch," but it wasn't. My mind was too far gone because of all the dope I was doing. The incident with the lab in his trunk was the first time my uncle ever really spent any time in jail, despite him being previously arrested several times. My Nanny had always gotten him out of everything. This time she let him go. She had to. Momma had already given the bank a portion of her disability settlement to keep them from foreclosing on Nanny's house, even though we desperately needed the money to get a place of our own and a vehicle (We had neither at that point in time). Nanny had already borrowed so much against her house to keep Nick out of trouble in the past that the bank was close to instigating foreclosure proceedings. Nanny was still able to use her property to bond Uncle Nick out of jail following his arrest, but she didn't have the cash to hire a lawyer and keep him out of jail.

After Uncle Nick was bonded out of jail following his arrest, I got kicked out of Nanny's house because there were all kinds of people coming in and out all hours of the night. Momma had found needles, too, but the main reason I was kicked out was because of my boyfriend, Luke. I kept letting him come over and stay after I was told he couldn't stay anymore. He was married the whole time we were together, and the worst part is that, at one time, his wife and I had been friends.

It was actually Momma, not Nanny, who kicked me out of the house. She told me that I was allowed to come there to eat or sleep, but that was it. They knew I didn't do much of either. I had gotten down to eighty-five pounds. Because of my meth addiction and the horrible lifestyle that came with it, I had gotten so small and under-nourished that, when I went to the doctor, the nurse practitioner said my liver was swollen and in such bad shape that I shouldn't even take a Tylenol or an over-the-counter stomach pill.

My veins got in such terrible condition that I started having trouble shooting up. I ended up in the hospital once because, when I tried to shoot up in my leg, I missed the vein. It got infected and looked awful. My leg got red and hot, and a big abscess formed on the side of my thigh. It was almost the size of a softball. It was nasty and scary. It just kept getting bigger and hotter until, finally, I went to the hospital. They gave me a shot of antibiotics, wrote me a prescription for additional antibiotics, and sent me to the house. I'm sure they knew what I had done. It was obvious I was using the needle. The doctor said that cellulitis had developed in my leg. To this day, I have a bulge on my left thigh due to this incident, but thankfully and miraculously, I still have my life.

Nanny felt sorry for me and let me come back home. That only lasted about a day. I let Luke come over and got kicked out again. I was so mad. I cussed everybody. Uncle Nick finally told me it was time for me to go (He hadn't been sentenced yet and was living at Nanny's). I was really hurt because I was just nineteen years old, and I was getting kicked out of the house for doing the same thing Nick was doing—and he was thirty-one. The only difference between me and Nick was that he wasn't in a relationship with Luke. Now, I see the issue—he was still legally married—but it hurt me tremendously at the time.

I hate to seem so rude and blunt here because I love my family dearly, but it's not like any of them had really taught me that this wasn't okay. It seemed like, just at the time when my lifestyle was really catching up with me, and I was spiraling out of control, they chose to ditch me and kick me out instead of trying to help me. Despite the obvious mess that I was in, no one offered to take me to get help or send me to a shelter of some kind. Instead, they just put me on the streets, which effectively meant that they sent me right back to my dealers.

See, that's the hard thing about being a young, pretty girl; it opens the wrong kind of doors. Please understand that I'm not boasting in any way; I never thought I was all that and a bag of chips, but I also knew I wasn't ugly and that all I had to do was "hang out" with the right guys and I could get pretty much all the dope I wanted. So, that's what I did. I went from dope house to dope house. That's how I lived. I had pretty much been living that way anyway, but I did occasionally take little breaks to escape some of the craziness when I would go to my Nanny's. Now I didn't have that option.

I was really mad and really confused. I had been rejected and had someone or something chosen over me once again. As if you can't tell, I've had a lot of resentment to deal with when it comes to my mom's side of the family, but I believe you have to be real. The only way we heal is to be real. I don't think it's going to help me or anyone else that reads this book who may have a loved one struggling or may be struggling themselves if I sugarcoat the truth.

As I've been writing this memoir, I have come to realize not only how much resentment I have held toward so many people and how much deep-rooted shame I had myself, but I can finally see that what hurt the most was the *rejection*. I see now how I repeatedly felt rejected. See, that's how the devil works. He wants you to feel unwanted, to make you think nobody wants you or could ever want you because you are so unlovable, unacceptable, and totally messed up. The devil also works hard to convince you that you are unworthy of God's love. This manipulation can keep you from turning to your heavenly Father when those who, by the natural order of things, should love you and take care of you, fail.

For me, these feelings of rejection started at an early age with my daddy. Then, it spilled over to various boyfriends as they walked away, beat me, or cheated on me. Then, it happened with my mom, with her men and her crack addiction, and, finally, with my Nanny and my Uncle Nick. That was hard, really hard. The ones I loved the most had hurt me the worst, but the devil is a liar and the father of lies (John 8:44). The Bible plainly says that "I am fearfully and wonderfully made" and that God will give me double honor for my former shame (Psalm 139:4, Isaiah 61:7). It took me a long time to reach the point where I could accept this truth, but by the grace of God, I finally know who I am and whose I am.

I have to remember these people who hurt me were human, and they had been hurt themselves. They were very, very broken people, and they, too, were struggling with various types of addiction and, in some cases, mental illness. As one of my favorite ministers says, "Hurting people hurt people." I am also human and have hurt many people over the years. Thank God, He remembers that we are merely dust (Psalm 103:14). I need to do the same. I can see my humanness and my need for mercy and forgiveness. Therefore, I needed to give that same forgiveness to others. The Bible tells us that we must forgive to be forgiven (Luke 6:37).

The truth is we all have our own sad story. Life is not all peaches and cream for anybody. That's why there is only one just judge, and it is definitely not me. Only God knows why we do what we do; He knows what causes us to react the way that we do in certain situations, and He remembers all of our pain, every hurt, and every heartache. That's why and how He can be so merciful; He loves us that much! Thank you, Lord! Thank God that He looks on our hearts and not just our actions. The Bible says that man looks at the outward, but God looks at our hearts (Samuel 16:7). All we as humans see is what people do, but our merciful God sees why we do what we do. I believe this is why the Bible says, "[He] will have mercy on whom [He] will have mercy on, and [He] will have compassion on whom [He] will have compassion" (Romans 9:15, KJV).

Looking back at getting kicked out of my nanny's house, I can see now that my mother was actually trying to save my life by refusing to continue enabling me. However, I only got worse, which is what usually happens. A drug addict has to hit a bottom of some kind. We don't get clean when everything is going well. We don't normally get clean when everything is falling apart either. It is only when we get to the point where we either have to do something different or die that we consider the possibility of taking steps to deal with our addiction.

For a while, I wandered from cook to cook, dealer to dealer, dope house to dope house—as the old saying goes, "from pillar to post." That was my life as a nineteen-year-old, strung-out "needle-junkie." This was about the time one of the county deputies that we knew personally went to talk to Momma about me. He told Momma she was going to have to do something with me before they (law enforcement) did, so she did. All of my closest friends, family, and running buddies were getting busted. She knew it was serious and just a miracle I hadn't already been arrested for possession or worse. I guess maybe they knew I was just an addict and a runner, not a big-time participant in the supply chain of the meth world. At that time, I don't remember many of the "smaller" people getting busted. They were going after the main cooks. It was still just by the grace of God that I hadn't been caught right along with them while we were buying materials, transporting labs, or cooking meth.

Even if they had arrested me for dope, I don't think they could ever have done anything worse to me than what I was doing to myself. It may have actually saved my life because I was slowly killing myself and, in such torment, mentally, that it was crazy. I was in a self-made prison (The thought of my childhood toy monkey in his little cage occurs to me once again). I was spiritually, mentally, and emotionally bound by addiction, shame, guilt, torment, paranoia, and so many other things I can't even begin to list them all.

We always thought the cops were out to get us, and although the drugs made us paranoid, we were not totally wrong. We tripped on the DEA, FBI, TBI (state bureau of investigation), and all of those big-name agencies. Later, we found out that there was a good reason to worry; we weren't just totally "geeked out" because David's trailer was eventually raided. Danny and Luke were both busted more than once, and I'm talking about the big agencies (not just county cop kind of raids).

They caught David with a lot of dope, and he was all alone. Nobody else could take the rap this time (It had been David's lab that got my Uncle Nick arrested). Luke and Danny had taken the rap for him more than once, too, to keep him out of trouble because he was the main supplier, the main source. Everybody knew that if David went down, it would put a hurting on our drug supply, and it did. I think someone from the inside had to be telling the authorities what David was doing because it just so happened to be the first time that I ever remember him cooking at his trailer alone.

The cops came in with haz-mat suits (like a hazardous materials clean-up crew). They had on white uniforms covering them from top to bottom. They had everything from the top of their heads to the bottoms of their feet covered, and they wore special masks because the fumes were so dangerous. They took David outside in his front yard, which was in the middle of town, stripped him down to his shorts, and sprayed him down with a water hose. Fumes from the cooking process to make meth are so harmful they can cause severe lung damage if inhaled. That's why they have to bring in haz-mat and all that. We used to make fun of the cops and say they were pansies because they were afraid of all the labs and the fumes. Of course, we were actually the ones who were stupid; it's like we had a death wish, and if the drugs weren't going to kill us, the cooking and the fumes would (Meth labs blow up on a fairly frequent basis, injuring or killing those who are unfortunate enough to be inside when it happens).

Looking back, it's really surprising that David didn't get busted before he did. The authorities must have been waiting to get him big and to get him alone so no one else would take the blame for him anymore, and that is exactly what they did. He went to the penitentiary for several years, along with Danny. David got more time than any of the other cooks that I knew.

Most of the cooks, big and little, were getting busted during that time period, but the meth world didn't slow down at all. The addicts just went to other places in the same county or moved over to another county to look for a fresh supply. The little guys who were left behind quickly became the big guys in the cooking world. A lot of addicts started trying to cook themselves, and the game continued.

Chapter Sixteen

Get Help

As soon as the county cop went to Momma, she came to me. She was extremely upset, and I was pretty upset myself. I was really freaked out, just to be bluntly honest. I had never been in any trouble over drugs before, but I was watching most of my closest friends go to jail because of meth. I was probably the most freaked out to know that I wasn't just a tripping paranoid mess but that the cops really had been watching me and had my number, so to speak. They knew not only who I was but where I was and what I was doing. To further complicate matters, the authorities had just started charging people with conspiracy in drug cases around our area.

I realize that conspiracy isn't a "new charge" per se, but it was a new charge related to drug use in our area. They were starting to charge people with conspiracy even though they were not the ones cooking, selling, or transporting meth; the police could, and often, did charge people with conspiracy to manufacture and/or distribute, just for being around those who were actually doing so. They had also started charging people with common exchange, meaning you could be charged just for using drugs with someone else. Meth had become such an epidemic in the area back in the late 1990s and early 2000s that the police would charge anyone who was involved in any way. They were just trying to get it under control in any way that they could.

I see now, once again, how God most definitely had His hand on me and was protecting me. I was extremely miserable at that time. I was wasting away to nothing; I weighed eighty-five pounds, my health was not good, and I was just nineteen years old. My mom took me to New Leaf Recovery at Plateau Mental Health Center, where I finally tried to get help, voluntarily, for addiction for the first time ever. They turned me away because I had TennCare insurance (Tennessee's version of Medicaid at the time), and the center couldn't accept me because my insurance wouldn't pay unless I said I was suicidal or homicidal. My mom knew that because she had worked there, but she didn't think to tell me until it was too late. I was too embarrassed to go back and say, "Yes, I'm suicidal," just so they would take me.

This is honestly a huge pet peeve of mine. Our health care system is broken in many ways, especially when it comes to mental health and substance abuse issues. You would think that someone who was nineteen years old, weighed eighty-five pounds, and had needle marks all up and down her arms could get some help without specifically saying she was suicidal (or homicidal). The truth was, I was slowly killing myself, but neither I nor the lady at the center thought of suicide in those terms. In all fairness, the lady I spoke to at the center tried to give me a second chance to tell her I was suicidal before she told me they couldn't help me, but I didn't say those magic words. I was too out of it at the time to realize that she was trying to tell me, through her facial expressions and repeated questioning, that I would have to say that I was suicidal in order to be admitted into the detox program. She really did try, but I just didn't know how the system worked.

I was an absolute broken mess inside and out. I even remember all these years later exactly what I was wearing and how I looked. As I'm typing, it's almost like I am on the outside of myself looking in. I had long hair then and had it all flipped up in a messy bun with my hair sticking out everywhere. I was wearing an old red ball shirt with black writing and a pair of black athletic pants with red stripes on the sides, and flip-flops. My clothes were just hanging off of me, my hair was a mess, and my arms looked especially awful. I had gotten past even trying to cover up my needle marks. So, there I sat, a broken, addicted, a teenage girl who was finally asking for help for the very first time in my life, but I couldn't get it because I didn't know enough to tell them what they needed to hear in order to have my (government-provided) insurance pay for the treatment.

This is when my momma sent me to my friend Linda's house (Linda was the friend I got in trouble with back in high school when I refused to beat up the pregnant girl but got arrested anyway). Her mom let me stay with them so I could try to dry out. Living with them for a while also got me out of the area where most of my using buddies and suppliers were located. Linda's family lived in Jackson County, away from most of the people, places, and things I needed to steer clear of. I knew a few people and connections in that area but not well enough to go to their homes, so I was fairly safe there.

Linda had been on meth herself right after we graduated from high school, but she had been straightened up for quite some time before Momma sent me to stay with her and her mom. She hadn't completely quit partying. She still smoked pot, but that was huge progress for her because she had been in pretty bad shape on meth like me at one point... except I don't think she ever shot up. Not that I know of, anyway.

As for quitting meth and the needle, was I ever in for a rude awakening. I went through withdrawals, something awful. Some people say you don't withdraw from meth. That's one of the biggest lies I have ever heard. The withdrawals were horrible. Still to this day, I have never gone through withdrawals as much or as bad I did when I was coming off of meth that first time. The cold sweats were terrible. I would freeze and chill but sweat at the same time. It was truly agonizing. I sweated so much, it was nasty, and it stunk really badly. I could smell myself. It was so gross, but that was my body's way of getting that junk out of my system. I can remember that smell now while thinking about it. It is a smell like nothing I can fully describe. It was almost like burnt rotten eggs with a strong chemical smell. The chemical smell overpowered everything else, and it smelled like the chemicals were seeping out of my pores (which, of course, they were). While this stuff was coming out of my body, I was crashing. All I did was sleep for days. I would get up to go to the bathroom and get a drink and maybe smoke a cigarette, and then I would crash again. I didn't even have enough energy to get off the couch. I think that was my body's way of catching up on all the sleep I had lost and trying to heal itself.

During this time, I never got completely clean. Once I got to the point where I could get off the couch, in the evenings, me, Linda, and her boyfriend would go riding around and smoke pot. I was taking nerve pills the whole time, too. Momma sent pot and nerve pills, Xanax to be exact, with me. Momma was afraid of what might happen if I didn't have something to help me come down. I know this sounds crazy to many people who may be reading this, but most from the drug world would understand. As a mother myself now, it's even hard for me to wrap my mind around it at times, but this was our lifestyle. It had become our norm for so long we didn't see anything wrong with what we were doing. To her, it was probably the equivalent of sending along a band-aid in case I got a blister walking around in my new shoes.

Momma legitimately thought that she was helping me by keeping me from going through full-blown withdrawals because withdrawals can actually kill you. They can cause you to go into seizures, can lead to a stroke or even heart failure. Giving me something to ease the withdrawal was all she knew to do to keep me from dying and get me off meth and the needle since I wasn't accepted into the treatment center. We both thought my only real problem was meth, my drug of choice, and the needle. We thought that, as long as I stayed away from meth and the needle, I could have a successful life—*wrong*. I see now how this was irrational thinking, but, at that time, it seemed right.

After I stayed with Linda for two weeks, I was sent to my dad's house in Virginia. If I remember right, that was the plan all along. I just had to get straightened up a little bit before I went. I didn't want to go to my dad's in that kind of shape. He had never seen me like that, and I didn't really know him or my stepmom very well at that time, certainly not well enough to go dry out at their house. I didn't want their first impression of me as an adult to be a "strung-out needle-junkie." I hadn't seen my dad since I had started using the needle. I think the last time I saw him was before my high school graduation a year or two earlier. Our relationship was still very strained, and our contact very sporadic.

Growing up, he would come through town in his big semi-truck and give me money every once in a while if he had a run where he could use I-40 to stop by and see me on his way through. Those were the only times I had seen him since I was very young. Sometimes, he would have time to stay a few minutes and eat with me at Hardees, a small, fast food joint near the interstate. We always met there because they had a place where he could park his eighteen-wheeler. Like I mentioned earlier, he quit coming to get me for visitations when I was six, not long after he remarried. He and his new wife, Gail, took me to see my Grandma Ollie in Virginia once after they married. I was around nine years old, so it had been over ten years since I had seen my stepmom or had stayed at my father's house overnight.

When I made it to my dad's in Virginia, I was still going through withdrawals. They weren't quite as bad, but they were still there, and I knew it. I hadn't kicked it yet, not physically or mentally. It was still pretty rough, but the sweating and most of that part was over. Momma sent weed and nerve pills again when I went to Virginia, so that eased the withdrawals that I was still experiencing. I only stayed there for two weeks, and I remember eating the majority of the time I was there. I ate and slept, ate and slept... I was still sleeping a lot at that time. I don't really remember much else. It was pretty much a blur, just withdrawals, pot, Xanax, food, and sleep. That was pretty much what those four weeks of trying to "dry out" consisted of.

After four weeks of being meth-free, I went back to Monterey, hoping I could go back home and make it. I really wanted to be with my mom and Nanny. I actually made it two whole weeks in Monterey without using meth, which was truly a miracle in and of itself, considering my previous situation and patterns of use (not to mention how prevalent the drug culture was in that little town at the time). I did continue to use pot and pills (that had never changed), but I stayed off of meth for a total of six weeks before I went back to it. The actual physical withdrawals had stopped, but the mental and emotional cravings had not. My desire to use was much stronger than my desire to not use.

A part of me realized that I felt a lot better overall when I was off the meth. I was finally starting to feel like myself again. I was even starting to feel better about who I was and how I looked, and how I acted. I wasn't so ashamed of myself anymore. I had put some weight back on and was looking more like my old self. I was actually thinking a lot more clearly, as well. I wasn't so crazy and paranoid. I was finally able to sit and have a normal conversation with people. For the first time in a long time, I could sit in the living room and spend time with my Nanny instead of hiding out in the bedroom all "geeked out" from meth.

Even though I was feeling much better and liked this new taste of a "meth-free" life I was experiencing, unfortunately, it wasn't enough to keep me away for very long. I was still bound, in a sense. There was still such a stronghold in me. I had never had anything get ahold of me like that before (nor have I since). Even though I was at my Nanny's house trying to do the right thing, all I could do was sit and think about meth and who I could go find to party with.

So, needless to say, I broke over and started using meth again pretty soon. I couldn't do it any longer (or, more accurately, I couldn't not do it any longer). I just did not have the strength, on my own, to stay away from crystal meth. I went right back to my drug of choice, my love—the only thing I had known for so long that brought me such peace and comfort yet such misery, despair, and destruction at the same time. You would think it would be different after being off of it for six weeks, but it wasn't. I still needed just as much to get high. Nothing had changed, except I was somewhat afraid of the needle after having been off of it for a while. I thought I could maintain and not get strung out or in trouble if I could stay away from the needle, but it was inevitable. My patterns would resurface, and I would go back down the exact same road again.

I was doing nothing to better myself or to keep from using, other than trying to stay away from certain people, places, and things. I hadn't replaced my bad behavior with anything positive. If you take something negative away, you must replace it with something positive, or else the devil has an open invitation to come right back in. If the hole is filled in, it's not so easy for him to get back in, but, of course, I didn't know that back then.

I believe this to be true with anything negative. If you take something negative out, you must replace it with something positive to fill that void. Otherwise, the negative thing—or something even worse—will re-fill that hole. This is just like where Jesus speaks about the unclean spirit that is cast out of a person. The spirit comes back with seven more spirits worse than itself when the original unclean spirit returns and finds the house swept, empty, and clean (Matthew 12:44-45). The key is to fill the house, the person, with something good, so the house is not empty when the spirit comes back. The person is the house, the temple of the Holy Ghost, and we must stay filled with God's Word and the Spirit of God so as to keep the negative things/spirits (demons) from coming back into our lives.

I did none of that. I just stayed at my Nanny's house using pot and pills and attempting to use willpower to keep from using crystal meth, one of the most highly addictive substances known to mankind. Very shortly, I went right back to using methamphetamine. Big surprise, huh? One day, I just couldn't take it anymore and took off walking across town to find something, and I did, immediately (That's how pervasive the drug culture was in my hometown at that time. Less than ten minutes, and I found what I was looking for). I didn't go straight back to the needle. I just snorted and smoked at first, but it didn't take long for me to go back to my real addiction and escape: the needle.

I didn't stay in Tennessee very long, maybe a few months, and then Momma sent me back to my dad's in Virginia before I had a chance to get totally strung out again. Things were already getting pretty bad, but I was not yet to the point that I had been before I had tried to dry out. The addiction had already gotten ahold of me just like before, except this time, it happened a lot faster. It's like I picked up right where I left off. I was living with dealers and cooks again and using just as much as I was before. I was doing anything and everything I could get my hands on. I was fully and completely addicted to meth and the needle once again.

Chapter Seventeen

A Second Chance

I was still just nineteen years old when I went to my dad's house in Virginia for the second time. Once again, I took some of Momma's pot and nerve pills (Xanax) with me because she wanted to make sure I didn't get "sick" from not having anything. It did keep me from going through full-blown withdrawals that time around, but I still had some pretty severe symptoms. For some reason, I remember a lot more about the withdrawal and recovery process during that second attempt to give up crystal meth.

I started going through withdrawals almost as soon as I got to Virginia. I don't remember "sleeping it off" like I had the first go-around. This time was much more difficult for me mentally and emotionally and, in some ways, even physically. I remember, very vividly, lying on my bedroom floor at night. I would be curled up in a ball in the fetal position, crying like a baby and singing lullabies to myself. That was the only comfort I could get. I was hurting, and the hurt was deep. It was beyond natural pain; it came from much deeper within. Every part of me hurt, inside and outside. I hurt mentally, emotionally, and physically in a way I could never truly explain. I missed my drugs, I missed my momma, and I missed my friends. I missed that old life. As bad as it was, that life was comforting to me because it was the only life I had known for so long. I suppose the lullabies reminded me of the last time I had really felt safe and secure in my life: back when I was just a little girl, being cradled in my momma's arms while she would sing to me.

I knew that the way I had been living was no good for me, but I still missed it terribly. It was all I knew. I know I am repeating myself, but I feel this is a point that needs to be reiterated and fully expressed: unless someone has dealt with addiction and lived that kind of life for a long period of time, I don't know that they could fully understand it. It becomes your normal. It becomes what brings you peace. It becomes what brings you comfort. Although it is completely chaotic and totally dysfunctional, it's what you are used to, what you have grown accustomed to, and what is familiar to you.

Anything outside of my "norm" was very uncomfortable for me on so many different levels, and, truthfully, at that time, the drug life was still very exciting to me. I had grown used to that life of chaos, and I missed it. Now that I had peace and quiet while living in the mountains of Virginia, I didn't know what to do with myself. Eventually, I began to learn, and, to my surprise, I really started to enjoy myself. I began to like the idea of having a fresh start and a new life. I started to dream again. I started to get my ambitions back. I started to want to really live again, which is something I had not truly done in a very long time.

My dad and Gail, my stepmom, lived up on this absolutely beautiful mountain in a really nice home, right below the airport in Vansant, Virginia. It was the very last home, way out away from everyone else and situated right on the side of the mountain. In fact, it was almost at the very top of the mountain. Our driveway was the last one on the left before you got to the airport. The view was amazing. I had never lived anywhere that nice before. It was so beautiful, peaceful, and out away from everyone else. It was absolutely gorgeous there.

They had a male dog, a Husky named Bo-Duke. He was so pretty, and he absolutely loved the snow. He was my new buddy. I had gone from living a wild life with a bunch of wild people to living in the middle of nowhere—a beautiful nowhere. I was used to living in town and being part of the party scene. There was none of that going on around me there in the mountains of Virginia. My dad was sixty-four, and my stepmother was in her fifties. They were pretty cool for their age. They still liked to live life, but they didn't party (use drugs), so I was still kind of lost in that regard.

This was a whole new life for me. Oddly enough, it was the dog, Bo-Duke, who helped me begin to find myself again. Through playing outside with him, especially in the snow, I began to find that child within that I had lost somewhere along the way through trauma, drugs, and alcohol. I was actually having fun for the first time in a long time, and it was nothing like my so-called "fun" when I was using meth and other drugs. Even though I was still smoking pot and taking a few Xanax, this was the "cleanest" my body had been—and the clearest my mind had been—since I was twelve years old.

The Lord tried to reveal Himself to me during that time in more than one way. One of the nights I was on my bedroom floor still going through severe withdrawals, I saw an airy white figure, full of light, floating up in the corner of my room. I believe now that it was an angel, possibly the angel of the Lord, but I didn't know what was going on then. Sadly, I ignored it because I thought I was hallucinating from previous drug use, but now I know I wasn't. I really believe it was an angel because I have had different encounters since being saved, and this one still sticks out vividly in my mind. I remember it catching my attention and making me feel better, but I didn't understand what was going on and just went on crying, rocking, and singing lullabies to myself on the floor.

There were other ways the Lord was trying to draw me to Him, as well. Even though I didn't understand it at the time, it's very clear now. Lori, my childhood friend, bought me a Bible with my name engraved on it. A guy I graduated with and was very good friends with was going to a Christian college, and we talked regularly on the phone. My stepmom and I discussed going to church, but we never followed through. I did sometimes read the Bible Lori bought me, and I tried to pray, but I just didn't really "get it." I just didn't understand that the Lord was drawing me to Him, and I really didn't understand what I read in the Bible, either.

I started really getting to know my dad for the first time that I could really remember. I was a Daddy's girl when I was little, but I didn't remember a lot about him except that he had to work all the time. This time I was getting to know him as an adult instead of as a child, and it was completely different.

Once I had been off the meth for a while, I started looking for a job. I was feeling the best I had felt in years physically, mentally, and emotionally. I was really starting to feel good inside and outside. I was feeling good about myself, my life, and where I was going. I was getting my hopes and aspirations back again. I decided that I needed to get a job (my first real job ever, by the way) and maybe go back to school and take some college classes. My dreams and goals were starting to come back to life again, and I was seeing that I could really do it, that I could overcome the addiction to meth and have a normal life.

My first job was at Issues & Answers, a telecommunication facility. I wasn't very good at it at all, so I got sent home early all the time. I didn't have to sell anything, but I had to make a certain number of completed surveys. I didn't make that quota very often, so that job didn't last long, but it gave me a chance to spend some time alone with my dad while he drove me back and forth to work.

My dad was able to drive me because he was off from work at that time due to problems with his eyes. As it turned out, my dad just so happened to be one out of a million whose cholesterol medicine caused double vision. I don't believe God caused his eye problems, but I do believe God used it to give us some time to get to know each other again. The double vision was clearing up by the time I moved in with Daddy that second time, but he stayed off work with me until I got settled.

The travel time to my job was about thirty minutes each way. They sent people home early almost every night. The ones with the least amount of surveys were sent home first. So, needless to say, I was sent home early almost every night. There were times that Daddy barely made it home before he had to come back and get me. He was driving about two hours a night to get me back and forth to work. At the rate I was going, my paycheck didn't even cover his gas. He wasn't letting me pay for his gas, but I still felt bad that he was driving so much and I wasn't making that much, so I quit that job, and Daddy took me around town looking for a job closer to home.

I had never worked before, so when I got that first payday at Issues & Answers, it felt really good. Even though it wasn't much, it was a big deal to me. I had never had a paycheck before. I had always lived off of my family and friends—or cooks and dealers when I was using. This new way of life felt nice. I was determined to get a job and work. I really liked the idea of working and getting paid for it. All I had ever received for any work I had done in the past was drugs. It felt great to have a real payday (No, I didn't spend any of the money on drugs). The only drugs I did at the time were what I got from my mom when she came in to visit. I would make them last until she came again.

I never really had any trouble getting a job. Now, I can see it was the favor of the Lord, but then I just thought I had good luck. When Daddy took me to town looking for a job closer to home after I quit Issues & Answers, I put in applications at most of the fast-food restaurants and Food City, the local grocery store. That very same day, Dairy Queen called me back, and I went right to work.

When I first started, I worked the night shift. I ended up working different shifts later on, but once I got the hang of things, they put me on the closing shift most of the time. I actually liked my job. I liked to stay busy. It made time go by faster, and you definitely stay busy at a fast-food restaurant! I think I started out making $5.25 an hour. For each new thing I learned to do, I got a raise. I learned to work the treat center, close, run the register and the drive-thru, but I never learned how to cook the food. It was already hot enough in there in the summer, and I wasn't about to go to that kitchen to roast for a few more cents on the hour. Plus, I didn't trust myself not to burn myself or something else up. I didn't know how to cook at that time. The only thing I had cooked outside of the microwave or sticking a pizza in the oven was dope. Obviously, the Dairy Queen had no use for my previous experience in that area.

I liked being out front better, anyway. I've always been a people person and liked social interaction. It was kind of fun. It was my new social life. It took the place of the social aspect of the drug scene. Most of the people who worked the night shift were young, some my age and some even younger. You get a lot of high school and college kids on the night shift coming in to work after school. We had a lot of fun goofing off and playing around when we didn't have a lot of customers in the restaurant.

There were quite a few older men and even a couple of older women who came into the Dairy Queen a lot. Most of them came in daily, and some of them came in more than once a day. They didn't work there, but they were there just as much, if not more, than most of the workers. They were our "regulars." They would come in the morning, eat breakfast, and then sit around drinking coffee and smoking cigarettes for hours. It's a common thing to do in small towns in the South, although each town has its own hang-out place for such a crowd. Some people jokingly refer to it as "holding court."

Those same older men and women would come back in the evening. Most of the time, they didn't even eat; they just sat around drinking coffee and smoking cigarettes. I guess this was their social scene, too. Most of them would go on with you about something all the time, just trying to get a laugh or rise out of you.

There were three of those older guys who were brothers. They were the Sexton men. I had gotten to know them all pretty well, and a few of their sons would come in and eat with them in the evenings. One of the older Sextons was named Jim, but everyone called him

"Blow Bag" because he was always blowing about something; you never knew whether to believe what he was saying or not. He loved to joke and cut up. Lots of times, he just made stuff up, and the stories that did have some truth to them, he blew all out of proportion. I loved him. He was hilarious and always going on about something.

His son, Jamie, was one of the younger guys that would come in and eat after work sometimes. I thought he was pretty cute. I guess you could say he most definitely caught my eye. I still remember what he was wearing the first time I saw him. He had on his work boots, Wrangler blue jeans, a white thermal shirt with a blue, short-sleeved pocketed t-shirt over the top of it, and a baseball cap.

I didn't take his food order, but he came back for dessert, and I got him that time. I don't think I was very inviting because I had somewhat of an attitude. My attitude wasn't necessarily directed toward him but rather to my friend, Brandy. She was the shift manager. She always bossed me around. That was just her natural attitude and her job. I was used to it for the most part, but this time she embarrassed me in front of Jamie. He ordered a Butterfinger Blizzard. I was already putting it together, getting ready to mix it, when she told me he had ordered a Snickers Blizzard. So, I turned to Jamie and said with quite a bit of attitude, "Hey, buddy, you did want a Butterfinger, didn't ya?" Not a very good first impression, I'm sure, but I was right; he had ordered a Butterfinger Blizzard. So, I fought through the embarrassment, finished the Blizzard, and gave it to him.

While he was still there, I told the girls that I worked with that I thought he was cute. I hadn't dated anyone since I had been in Virginia, and I had been there for a few months. I was honestly trying to keep to myself and stay out of trouble. The night shift manager lived up the same holler (slang for a hollow, a miniature valley in the mountains where most of the side roads are in Virginia) as Jamie's dad, Blow Bag. She said that Jamie had always been a good boy and worked hard. The fact that Jamie was supposed to be a good guy and a hard worker was amazing to me. None of the guys I had dated before had held down a real job. If they worked at all, it was only long enough to get a good payday and get high, or they made their "living" cooking and selling dope.

Once Jamie left, my coworkers told his dad, Jim, that I thought his son was cute. Now, you have to remember, his dad was one of those older Sexton guys who hung out at the restaurant all the time, and he loved to joke around. He came up to the front counter and started teasing me and asking me where I was from. I think he already knew, but I told him again. He always went on and on about my coal-black eyes and said my eyes were like Jamie's mother's. He then went on to tell me that Jamie wanted my number, but I was too embarrassed to give it to him myself. I went and hid out in the drive-thru because I was so embarrassed, so Brandy gave my phone number to him.

Jim (a.k.a. "Blow Bag"), Jamie's dad, took my number and gave it to Jamie. Jamie was staying at his mom's house at the time. He didn't even remember which worker I was. That should've been a definite sign that Jim had lied about him wanting my number, but I didn't catch on.

Later, when we had been dating for several months, and things had gotten serious enough that I took him to Tennessee to meet my Nanny, the truth came out. I was telling my Nanny how Jamie wanted to go out with me, and he was trying to tell her how I wanted to go out with him. It was a bit of an argument, and then we realized what ole "Blow Bag" had done. He had set us up. He told me Jamie wanted to go out with me and wanted my number. He then took my number to Jamie and told him I gave him my number and wanted to go out with him. This was one thing I can say I'm glad he lied about. He may have fibbed just a little or a whole lot, but either way, it all worked out in the end. When Jamie got back home, he confronted his dad about what he had done, and he said, "I done good, didn't I?" and busted out laughing with his silly, sly laugh.

But he was right. He had "done good." Jamie and I hit it right off when we first started dating. It was almost like an instant connection. He told me that he had always wanted a girl from "far away." So, here I was, his dream girl, and he was most definitely my knight in shining armor. He was so sweet, a real gentleman. He even opened the car door for me. I was amazed. He really spoiled me. He took me shopping, out to eat, and to the movies all the time. He bought me all kinds of clothes and even a few small pieces of diamond jewelry (diamonds just so happen to be my birthstone). I was actually dating a guy who worked a real job and treated me like somebody for the first time in years.

I still remember our very first date and even what each of us was wearing. He couldn't find our house, so my dad met him out at the Fire Department right below our place. He had a little white Nissan truck, and he was wearing a gray No Fear shirt with Levi's and a baseball cap. I was wearing a mustard-colored tank top with a white three-quarter-length button-up shirt over the tank, but I left it unbuttoned. I had on jeans and some really cool clogs with flowers on the heels. They were very hippie-like—totally, always my style.

Jamie picked me up at the Vansant Fire Department and took me to Claypool Hill to the movies and then out to eat. The movie theater was in the Claypool Hill Mall. He was so sweet and shy that he wouldn't even hold my hand. I had to grab his hand as we were walking through the mall. He was so sweet and such a gentleman. I wasn't used to that. When he dropped me off at my dad's, he didn't even try to give me a goodnight kiss. I had to kiss him. I know this is a little mushy, but y'all remember how it is when you're young and in love, especially the first time you ever really have a true gentleman take you out. It's just amazing. Thinking back on it makes me all giddy, and I fall in love all over again. He is truly one of a kind. God did "real good" when He made him!

Jamie was a great guy all around. He worked and didn't do drugs, and he treated me like somebody, which is something I wasn't used to. Some of his friends partied, and he had tried drugs, but he never really liked it or developed a problem with drugs. He mostly just drank a little beer when we went out. I had never really dated anyone who did not use at least some kind of illegal substance, not since I was in elementary school, anyway. It was a welcome change.

He knew I partied a little. I told him I smoked some pot, and I drank with him every once in a while. I told him the truth about my past, the needle and all. He was very understanding and knew I was trying to live better. The thing that he didn't know was that I was still sneaking around and taking pills. Although I had started to fear the drug life because of how much I was enjoying things there in Virginia, where I was relatively clean, I had not totally given it up. Unfortunately, I was about to find out that my "recovery" was much more fragile than I realized.

Chapter Eighteen

Hanging on by a Thread

In 2001, as soon as I started working, I started saving money to buy a car. At the age of twenty, once I had saved enough for a decent down payment, tags, and insurance, I went car shopping and found a little green Chevrolet Cavalier that I just loved. It was super cute, really cheap on gas, and kind of sporty. They were asking somewhere around $3,800 for it. Daddy offered to buy it for me, but I said no. I thought I needed to learn how to do things on my own. I had never worked or paid bills at that point in my life. I had never had any type of responsibility, to be honest. I had always depended on my mom for everything. My dad offered again to buy the car for me right in the parking area of the car lot, but Gail, my stepmom, was sure to let him know I had already said no.

Daddy did offer more than once, but I didn't accept. I wanted to do it for me. I was proud of myself. I had bought my first car, and it felt good. Actually, it was not the first car that I had ever had, but it was the first car that I had bought for myself with money that I had earned. It was a completely different experience than buying a car using money from my Pell Grant (the federal funding I received to go to college) when I was still living in Tennessee. I had worked this money out myself and worked hard to save it and not spend it. It wasn't just handed to me. Momma may have given me a little money here and there, but for the most part, I had worked for it and saved it all by myself. I believe everyone needs to learn to work for what they want if they are able. If everything is just handed to you, you will expect it, and you will never appreciate anything or learn to stand on your own two feet.

Once I got my car, I paid my car payment and car insurance every month. I never remember having to ask for help with it. I gave my car insurance money to Gail every month because I was on her and Daddy's insurance. They co-signed for the car, but I had the payment book, and I paid it myself at the bank. I began to feel self-respect and self-worth for the first time in my life. There were a few times I was running low on money and would have to get Jamie to buy my cigarettes, but I always paid my own bills. Sometimes I just didn't have enough money for the extras, but Jamie didn't mind. He always offered. He liked helping me and taking care of me.

Around the time I bought my car, a girl named Mia started working at Dairy Queen with me. She had gone to school with Brandy, and they were the same age. They were both about a year younger than me. Mia was a little bit wilder than we were, at least wilder than I was at that time. I started hanging out with Mia quite a bit, and Jamie didn't like it. He never really cared for her. I guess he knew she was a bad influence. Mia not only drank alcohol and used drugs, but she really liked the guys, too. She was engaged to a guy named Corey, but he wasn't the only one she was with at the time, and everyone knew it.

At first, we just got out and smoked a little weed. Then, one night Mia and I went to Council, a small town about thirty minutes away from Vansant (where I was living in Virginia). One thing led to another, and we ended up hanging out with a couple of Mia's friends (a guy named Pepper and his dad). I had never met them before. We went to their house with intentions to smoke some weed, but they had crank (It is probably not giving anything away to say that I am getting ready to take a wrong turn here shortly; if you have read this far, you should be starting to see a pattern).

I actually said no to the crank at first. I was truly scared of going down that same road again, and I had to work the next day. But Mia talked me into doing it. She said she didn't want to do it alone because she had never done it before. Truthfully, it didn't take much persuasion because a part of me had truly missed my drug of choice, crystal meth (Crank is just a dirty, less pure form of crystal meth). Even though part of me had missed that high, another part of me didn't want to do it. It's like there was a war going on within me. It was almost like the little angel on one shoulder and the little devil on the other shoulder in the cartoon captions you see; that was very much what it felt like. I had done so well by staying away from what I thought to be "hard drugs." In my mind, I was clean because I was just smoking weed, drinking a little, and taking a few pills.

I was scared to touch those "hard drugs" because I knew what they had done to me before. I knew what a hold they had on me. I knew how they had destroyed my life and how awful I felt about myself when I was on them. With a tiny bit of peer pressure, however, the little devil won the battle that time, and the little angel on my shoulder lost its fight this go around. Deep down, I think I knew I was starting to go down the wrong road again, and I really didn't want to see Mia go down that road either. I think I was more worried about her than I was about myself because I had seen what happened to young, attractive girls in the drug world, and I knew what she was getting ready to do and the dark turn that her life was about to take. She hadn't been on any hard drugs yet at that time. She had never really had an addiction of any sort, but that was soon to change.

We ended up staying at Pepper's house all night long. I went on to work the next morning and worked my shift, despite having gotten no sleep at all. Afterward, I went to Jamie's and crashed. I hadn't done all that much crank that night (relatively speaking), just enough to make me feel really bad about myself and worry about Mia. Pepper's dad said he thought I had my head on straight. I wish he had been right about that. I guess that maybe compared to Mia, who was just starting to go wild, I seemed more sensible than I really was. I had already been down the road that she was just starting on, and I knew where it would lead.

Around the time I turned twenty, Daddy and Gail moved to Raven, Virginia, a town about thirty minutes from where we had been living. I moved with them. I soon found a job at the Dollar Tree in Claypool Hill, Virginia. I actually helped them set the store up and open it. This would have been in the late summer of 2001. I remember it vividly because the national 9/11 tragedy occurred while we were in the process of setting up the store. Not long after the store opened, I was promoted to Third Key Associate Manager. I had also gone back to college and was doing well in school. I managed to pull my grades up and make the Dean's List while working at the Dollar Tree and doing work-study. I stayed on the go all the time. I was working, going to college full-time, and doing work-study. It looked like I was going to excel this time. On the surface, I appeared to have it all together.

It looked like I really had it going on this time. Jamie and I had even gotten engaged and moved in together. We were doing well as a couple, but we thought it was a good idea to live together before we got married (Remember, neither of us was saved at that time). I know now that this was not a good idea for more than one reason, but at the time, it saved us from a divorce.

Jamie and I rented a small, older house in the middle of Richlands, Virginia, less than ten minutes away from my dad and midway between where Jamie and I worked. We happened to move in straight across the road from my aunt, uncle, and cousin. This was really just a disaster waiting to happen. I have previously shared with you about my mother's side of the family, but this was my daddy's family, my dad's sister, her husband, and her son. My aunt didn't drink or do drugs, but my uncle and cousin both did.

Once we moved so close to them, I finally got up enough nerve to ask them to hook me up with some weed, pain pills, and a few nerve pills. I had also gotten brave enough to ask a guy at school to get me some weed and pills. I had a class with him. He sat right in front of me and always came in stoned and reeked of weed, so I knew he had the hook-up. You know, it's like they say, "You will find what you're looking for." You could have taken me (or anyone else on drugs) to any place in the world, and it would not have taken me long to find drugs and start partying if that's what I was looking for... and that is what I was looking for. At this point, I had to find connections, not just one, but more than one, to keep me in a constant flow. My addiction was getting ahold of me again.

It was really starting to take over my life, but I couldn't see it—at least not yet. I was nervous about finding new connections, about asking around for drugs when I didn't know people very well and didn't know who I could trust. Back in Tennessee, I knew most of the people in the drug scene and thought I could trust them. Now, I was in a different state and didn't know who I could trust and who I couldn't. Still, I had started running out of dope before Momma's visits, and I had to do something in an attempt to hold me over. At least that's what I told myself.

In reality, I was starting down a whole new road of addiction, one that would take me to a place that I had never been before. Yes, I had dealt with addiction in several forms by this point in life—addiction to meth, to nerve pills, to cocaine—but I was getting ready to go down the road of opiate addiction, a road that I was most definitely not prepared for or educated about. I had no idea what was in store. All I knew was I didn't have enough of what I needed to hold me over anymore. I was starting to need more and more drugs, and I was determined to get them.

As you can see, I was heading down a one-way street in the wrong direction at a high rate of speed. Then, as if on cue, there came Momma. She had gotten strung out on crack again and gotten into some trouble for writing bad checks. She called me to bail her out of the mess that she had made for herself. I had been saving money for quite a while for Christmas and a trip to Tennessee. I think it was around

$1000, which was a significant amount of money to me at the time. I agreed to give her what I had, but on one condition: she had to come and stay with me in order to get the money. I refused to mail it to her because I was afraid she would use it on drugs instead of what it was intended for. I made her come to Virginia, and then she sent the money back to Tennessee to pay off the bad checks. I didn't tell Jamie what was going on. I just told him that Momma needed to stay with us for a little while until she could find work. I never told him she had been strung out or had gotten in trouble again. So, there I was, twenty years old, bailing my momma out of trouble again and even lying about it to my fiancé, the only man who had ever treated me right in my entire life. Yes, things were heading toward a definite downward spiral; so, here we go!

I was afraid that if I told Jamie the truth, he would not want Momma to stay with us. I was also afraid that he would think she was a bad influence on me, which was true, but I was the bad influence on her life at many times. We had a very dysfunctional relationship, but I always loved my momma, and I had missed her tremendously since I had been living in Virginia. I was tickled to have her nearby and was willing to do whatever I needed to do in order to have her with me. While I was really upset and angry with her for getting in trouble, I was happy that she was going to be close to me again.

Lori, my friend from back home, brought Momma to Virginia. Lori stayed and visited for a couple of days and then went back home. If I remember correctly, Lori knew what had really happened, at least most of what was going on, with Momma. I don't know if I told her I was having to bail Momma out of trouble, but I'm pretty sure she knew that Momma had gotten in bad shape again and needed to get away from Monterey. I'm not sure how I thought I would help her. I guess I did financially, and she didn't do any cocaine or crack-cocaine while she was in Virginia that I know of, but we were still a train wreck waiting to happen once we got back together because we enabled one another, so much. That's hard for me to admit. I don't know that I have ever admitted that I enabled my momma. I knew she enabled me, but I am just now seeing and admitting that I very much enabled her, as well. I can't believe I didn't see that, or maybe I didn't want to see it. Denial is a very tricky thing when it comes to addiction and enabling.

Needless to say, we started blowing it up with pot and pills. I was excited to have my momma back, but, if I'm honest with myself, I think I was almost as excited—and even more relieved—to have her drugs back. For years, she had been prescribed my very favorite pain pill at the time, Xanax nerve pills. She was also prescribed Lortab pain pills, and she always managed to keep weed, the one thing I thought I would never quit. We smoked constantly. We would go riding around to smoke or smoke in the bedroom and stink up the whole house. Having Momma actively back in my life was the beginning of the end of my newfound "sobriety," such that it was.

At that time, I had never smoked pot in front of Jamie. He finally told me that he would rather I just did in front of him at home instead of going out riding around all the time. He didn't know what he was asking for. That just gave me a license to use. I didn't have to hide it anymore. I still hid the pills. I would snort them in Momma's room. I thought I had the perfect little set-up. There were two doors to Momma's room. I would have everything crushed and lined out in a plate in my mom's dresser drawer before he got home. I would go in one door, snort really fast, come out the other door, and then go get smoked-up in the living room. He had no idea that I smoked that much pot when he told me he would rather me do it in front of him. Drugs really scared Jamie. He had never really been into drugs, especially at the level that I was using them then.

Things quickly deteriorated to the point where I was hanging on to that life of relative normalcy by the barest of threads. From the outside looking in, I had it all together. I was engaged to be married, had a home, had a car, was on the Dean's List and in the Honor's Society, and was an assistant manager of a store. Considering all that I had been through in the past, those were all major accomplishments. However, if you could have seen things from the inside looking out, you would have seen a very messed up young woman on the brink of disaster.

Chapter Nineteen

Lying, Cheating, and Stealing

As I said earlier, Jamie drank a little here and there, but he didn't do drugs and had no idea what all I was doing. Once I started smoking pot in front of him, our relationship took a quick, sharp turn for the worse. He already knew I was acting crazy and had changed, but now he had an idea of why. He thought it was the weed, stress from school, stress from work, and Momma being there. What he didn't know about were all the pills I was doing.

I was getting out of control. Momma's pills were nowhere near close to being enough for me. Seeing as how they were her prescription medications, she was taking them, too, of course. I had to start buying stuff off the street just to keep me going. I had to have something to go to school. I had to have something to work. It was not just in my head, either; I had reached a point where, physically, I had to have the pills in order to function, period. My addiction had spun out of control that bad, that fast.

Jamie was always a good guy. He worked, he was dependable, and he was trustworthy. This was something totally new for me, something I knew nothing about and had never seen in a guy before. I always thought that if something seemed too good to be true, then it must be too good to be true. I tried to prove to myself that, deep down, Jamie was just like every other guy. I pushed every button he had, trying to push him over the edge. I would get out and party. I physically pushed him, cussed him, threw stuff at him, broke his stuff, and even hit him. During this time, I did pretty much anything and everything humanly possible to push him to his breaking point, but he never broke.

Every other guy I had dated had either cheated on me or beat me—sometimes, even both. I must have been trying to prove that Jamie would do the same, but he never did. He was faithful. This was something else totally new to me. This kind of relationship—this kind of man—was something I knew nothing about and didn't understand or appreciate at the time. He would get so mad at me when I would get in his face, cussing him or hitting him, but he would never hit me back. He would just walk away or leave. *What a man, huh!* At the time, it infuriated me that he wouldn't "fight back" like all the other men I had been with. It was the only life I had known, and I couldn't appreciate Jamie and the real man that he was. I couldn't appreciate anything at the time. The only thing I could appreciate even for a moment was a joint or a pill.

I even tried to make Jamie believe he was an alcoholic to keep from looking at me when he would try to confront me about my problem. Whenever he would try to talk to me about smoking so much pot and what he thought it was doing to me, I would throw a fit, throw a pity party, or throw it back at him. I would just totally lose it and throw a temper tantrum like a child (Yes, the figurative monkey in the cage was back in my life, big time). I would tell him how awful my life had been and that if he had been through all I had been through, then he would get high, too. I would even try to make him think he was an alcoholic to get him to leave me alone. In my mind, if he had a problem, then I didn't. As long as he was the problem or had a problem, then I didn't have to look at myself as being the problem or look inside myself to see what a mess I was.

They say that if a train is wrecking, you had better jump off. Well, I was a train wreck about to happen, and it was high time that Jamie jumped off before I pulled him down with me and wrecked his life, too. After being together for over two years (I was twenty-one years old by that point), we had finally reached a place in our relationship that he had taken all he could from me, and he was not willing to take any more of my abuse. I respect him for that today, but at the time, it made me crazy mad. I could not handle rejection. It felt like the only man who had ever really cared anything about me was leaving me, but it was all my fault this time. For the first time, I couldn't blame anyone but myself. Jamie left me and moved in with his dad.

I began to take a major turn for the worse. I started partying hard. I had parties at the house all the time with all kinds of guys. I believe Jamie somehow kept me grounded, but he wasn't my keeper. As they say, "Everything happens for a reason." I had to hit rock bottom in order to realize I had a problem with *any and all* drugs, not just crystal meth and the needle. Within a few weeks of Jamie and me splitting up, I lost my job at the Dollar Tree. I also started shooting OxyContin (oxycodone hydrochloride), a very potent, prescription opioid medication that was originally formulated for the terminally ill. The first time I tried it, I was hooked. It wasn't very long before I was totally strung out again.

I was far from alone with regard to my rapid addiction to OxyContin. The United States Food & Drug Administration had approved oxycodone for prescription usage in the mid-1990s. Within a few short years, it had become the drug of choice for an entire generation of drug addicts, including many in the rural South. Like other pills, it could be swallowed, snorted, or shot into the arm via a needle. In some circles, abuse of oxycodone was so prolific that it became known as "hillbilly heroin." In the succeeding years, several other opioid medications (such as fentanyl) were also approved, worsening the problem. More recently, there has been a pushback against the over-prescription and general abuse of opioids, with several state attorney generals filing lawsuits against drug companies and the federal government launching multiple investigations into the pharmaceutical industry's culpability in the creation of the crisis.

Before I started using Oxy, I had not used the needle since I had left Tennessee two years earlier. Other than the one time that Mia and I used crank, I had not used street drugs like cocaine, meth, or crank at all during that same time frame. Even though I had managed to stay off the needle for over two years, it was about to destroy my life again. It happened really fast this time. I was already doing a pretty good job of destroying my life myself without the OxyContin, but once I started shooting Oxy, there was no turning that train back around. I was wrecking—and I was wrecking fast. You might say that the train was about to fully derail.

After Jamie and I broke up, I started dating another guy. He was a real gem; he totaled my dad's Jeep. I pawned everything I had—all of my jewelry (including my engagement ring), our TV, stereo, and anything else they would take—in order to get money to buy dope. I got kicked out of my house. I lost both of my cats. One went missing, and the other ran away from me at the post office. I guess I would have run away from me, too, if I could have. I loved that cat. He was a beautiful, solid gray cat named Blue, and I had raised him from a kitten. Jamie and I found him as a stray when he was tiny, and we cared for him like he was our child. I had him so spoiled that he even loved to ride in the car with me. He was the only cat I have ever known who liked to ride in the car. He stayed right with me all the time, but not anymore. It seemed like even the cat had a better sense of what was going on than I did at that point, and he knew he needed to get away.

After I lost both of my cats, I even traded my dog, Susie, for dope. She was a precious dachshund/ terrier mix but looked like a black long-haired weenie dog. I had gotten her when I was still in Tennessee. My mom had brought Susie with her when she was staying with Jamie and me. After I had lost my fiancé, my job, and my two cats, I traded my dog to a drug dealer for cocaine and pot. It was the dealer's little girl's seventh birthday, and he wanted the dog for a birthday present. I didn't really want to do it. I was hesitant, but I traded her because I was desperate for drugs. This is still very hard to talk about. This was one of my lowest points. I know it may sound crazy to some because of some of the other stuff I did that didn't really faze me, but my animals were like children to me. I really loved them, and it was really hard on me to lose them. I searched for my cats but never found them. I checked on Susie from time to time to make sure she was okay. I saw her once with the little girl, and she seemed really happy. I know a drug dealer's home was not a good place for her, but it was a better place than living on the streets with me. Thank God I didn't have children at the time. I hate to even think about what might have happened to them.

I wrote a bunch of bad checks during that time. Some were in my name (about $2000 worth), and some were using my daddy's name. I have no idea how much I wrote on my dad. He never told me, nor did my new stepmother, Jannie. My dad and his previous wife, Gail, had split up during my drug craze towards the end of my relationship with Jamie. After his divorce was final, he met Jannie. She was a great,

Christian lady. They were married not long after me and Jamie split up. To this day, they still have not told me how much money they spent to get me out of trouble, and, to be honest, I probably don't really want to know—not even now.

I wrote checks everywhere. I would get gas or cigarettes and then write the check for as much over the amount of the purchase as they would let me. Back then, most places would let you write it over anywhere from $10 to $35. Every day, I hit every convenience store that would let me write a check over the amount of the purchase. I also wrote bad checks in Wal-Mart and Food City. They were the same way. You could buy a pop (soft drink) and then write the check for $10 to $20 over the amount. I had to hit as many places as I could in a day just to get that fix. Those Oxys were outrageously expensive; eighties (an eighty milligram OxyContin) was what my main dealer had, and one pill went for anywhere between $80 and $120.

Of course, I was doing a little bit of anything and everything I could get my hands on, including cocaine, meth, and morphine, but Oxy had become my drug of choice at that time. I became so desperate to get money for a fix, I even went to Wal-Mart a few times, bought the most expensive electronics I could get out the door with, paid with a bad check, and then had my boyfriend-of-the-moment take the items back in the store and get a cash refund.

My dad and Jannie took care of the checks on his account. My mom was working for some wealthy people at the time in Roanoke, VA was able to pay off most of my bad checks. What she couldn't pay, Daddy covered. I had to pay the fees at the bank, pay the service charge at each store, and personally pick the checks up at the stores. It was so embarrassing going into those stores and picking up bad checks. My mom wouldn't do this one for me. She and Daddy covered the expenses to keep me out of jail, but they made me go in the store and pick up each check myself. Even then, I still couldn't stop. I was hooked, really bad, and I couldn't quit.

After all that, I still managed to find a way to get my hands on some checks. I was dating a guy named Brian, who had introduced me to Oxy. He and I went to Galax to visit my friend Brandy (my coworker from the Dairy Queen). While we were there, we went to a bank and picked up some counter checks. I cashed the checks, went back to Richlands, and got high again. Brandy knew about all the trouble my mom had just bailed me out of, so when Momma called, she told her what I had done. I got so mad at Brandy that I would not even talk to her for a couple of years. Now, I realize that she was a true friend and was looking out for my best interests. Thank God for good friends!

My mom was able to follow my tracks and clean up my mess once again. Bless her heart. She couldn't bear the thought of her baby going to jail, even though it might have been the best place for me at the time. After all that, I moved to Roanoke with my mom for the summer because I had lost my home. I got off of the Oxys for a while. Of course, Momma and I still smoked weed and did her Xanax and

Lortabs, but that was all—a huge change from what I had been doing.

After about a month, I went back to Richlands. I moved in with Brian at his mom's and got a job at Shoney's. I was still trying to go to college. The semester that Jamie and I split up, I had been given an academic warning. This semester, I officially flunked out. I couldn't go to school, work, and keep up my addiction. My days of being a "functioning addict" were almost over. Needless to say, my addiction was my first priority. I remember putting makeup on my arms to cover my track marks just so I could go to work. Then, I lost my job for trying to steal a candle topper. How stupid! But, by this time, I had more than one addiction. Not only was I a heavy drug user, I lied about everything, no matter how silly or minuscule it may have been. I didn't know how to tell the truth. I would also steal anything that was not bolted to the floor. Stealing had become an addiction in and of itself, the same way the needle had.

With the needle, I would get a rush as soon as I saw the blood draw back because I knew I was going to get high. With stealing, I got a rush every time I stole anything, no matter how small or silly it was—even a candle topper from a co-worker at Shoney's. I have no idea what I thought I was going to do with that topper. I didn't have a candle for it to go on; I didn't even have a home! All I had left was my car. I'm not sure why stealing was such a rush, but it was. It was nonsensical, but it was yet another thing I was hooked on. I had become an addict, a needle addict, a compulsive liar, and a kleptomaniac—and I wasn't even twenty-two yet.

Somehow, I actually managed to keep my car. I was awarded federal Pell Grant money for college each semester. I would use it to pay my car payment up until I got the grant money again. That's the only smart thing I did during that time, but it wouldn't matter for long.

Addiction had me once again. I was no longer my own. It owned me. I had lost all control. I was a physical, mental, and emotional train wreck waiting for a place to happen.

Chapter Twenty

Total Loss of Self Control

I continued to stay with Brian for a while in 2003. He worked a few odd jobs here and there but never anything steady, and it never lasted long. He would work just long enough to get a couple of good paydays. Then, we would get blown away on pills, and that would be the end of it. He wouldn't go back to his job. We lived at his mom's house for a while, but she kicked us out for fighting and, supposedly, because he wouldn't work. However, I think we really got kicked out more because of the fighting than because of him not working. They had let him stay there before when he wasn't working—and I was working at Shoney's the whole time we were living there. The fighting just kept getting worse.

Arguing, fighting, and abusive, combative relationships were the norm for me. If the guy didn't beat me or yell at me, then I was the one picking fights. I just had to have that chaos going, one way or another. With Brian, it wasn't him who was causing problems. Mostly, it was me. He was a small, skinny guy, and I used him like a punching bag. I had so much anger built up inside of me, and I took it out on anyone I could. He was an easy and seemingly willing target. He seemed to really love me and was willing to put up with whatever I did. He rarely fought back.

I really feel terrible about it now. I really had a lot of problems, but it wasn't right to take things out on him. It makes me feel really bad now to admit to my behavior during that relationship and to talk openly about it, but lying to myself does not help me or anyone else. It's the truth that sets us free, and many times that truth is not only the truth about Jesus and from the Word of God but also the truth about ourselves that will set us free. I have to see myself and my past as they truly were before I can really be free (The same goes for you, by the way). Denial does not help anyone. It only keeps us stuck. If we let God take us on a self-exploratory journey, we can find much healing through the revelation found within. All of my issues, my anger, my addiction, etc., were related to self-control—lack of self-control, that is. When I was with Brian, my lack of self-control caused us to be put out on the streets.

We tried staying at a few different places with different people we knew, but we didn't have anywhere steady to stay. We just stayed anywhere we could, even in my old house, which had been condemned after I was evicted. That tells you a lot about the kind of life I lived during that time period. The house was in good shape when Jamie and I lived there and even when he left me, but by the time I was done with it after I was back on the needle, the county condemned the place. I knew it was bad but not that bad. I had destroyed that house just like I was destroying my life and anyone else who was connected to me. One night, we were staying in that old house and had passed out after shooting morphine. We were awoken by a cop and my old landlord hollering for us to get out of there. The cop told us he could charge us with criminal trespassing, and if we did it again, he would. We left and didn't go back.

I don't really remember where we went next or what we did to survive after we were kicked out of my old house that night. A lot of what happened during that time is a blur. I'm sure my substance abuse contributed to the memory lapse, but I believe I subconsciously blocked some of it out, too. However, I do have one particular memory from that time that is one of the worst memories I have of my entire life. It happened at a time when I was completely lost. I really don't remember all that happened that night, but I know it was bad—really bad. It was one of the most shameful things to come from my many years as a drug addict, and it was one of the hardest things that I had to deal with years later when I got sober (Speaking personally, it is a lot easier for me to forgive other people and give them a break than it is to forgive myself. I carried guilt and shame over this event for many years. It was only through the grace of the Almighty that I was able to release all of that pain and move forward with my life).

Momma had been working in Tazewell, Virginia, but she had recently come back to the Raven area closer to where I was living. She was dating a guy named Kenny. It was the beginning of the month, and I knew Momma had gotten her disability check. I needed money, and I knew that she had money. It wasn't much, but it was still money, and I was desperate. Brian and I had been up the road shooting Dilaudid (Hydromorphone, another highly addictive, very potent opioid drug) and taking nerve pills. We ran out of Dilaudid. We were not far from where Momma was staying, so I walked to Kenny's mom's house and knocked. Momma came to the door. I asked her for money. She gave me a few dollars for cigarettes and gas, but it wasn't enough—nowhere near enough for what I wanted, which was, of course, more drugs. I started arguing with her to give me more.

Kenny's mom told me to leave and get off of her property. I got mad at Momma for letting her talk to me like that and for not giving me the money that I wanted. As the argument escalated, Momma started walking down the road. She was trying to get me away from his mom's house before I embarrassed her and/or Kenny's mother called the cops and I got in trouble.

When Momma walked away from me, I went into an absolute rage. It was as if I had blacked out or something because, to this day, I don't remember exactly what happened. What I do know is that, at that time, I could not stand for anyone to walk away from me. I would feel rejected all over again. I know that may seem silly, especially if the other person was just trying to avoid an altercation, but I couldn't see it that way. I had real issues. I thought that, no matter what I did to someone, if they loved me, they would just stand there and take it. Not rational, I know, but I was all kinds of messed up.

Momma kept trying to walk away from me. I chased her down and tried to take her money. I went crazy and started beating on her. I was told later that Brian even kicked her while she was on the ground. It makes me furious to even think of him hurting my momma, but I have to remember that he was in the same mental state that I was: we were two crazed drug addicts needing a fix.

I don't know many other details of this event. All I know is that I hurt my momma, both physically and emotionally, that night. Later, I would not only regret what I had done but would come to hate myself for it. The whole thing was like an out-of-body experience, like some demon had taken me over. Of course, a demon *had* taken me over—the demon of *addiction*! I had given it control of my mind, my body, and my soul. It is an absolute shame to see what drugs do to people. I wasn't a mean, evil person; I was just sick. Very, very sick. I really loved my momma, but you sure couldn't tell that at the time.

Some random, unknown guy passed by, saw what was going on, and called the police. The cops came and took me to jail. I ditched my needle in the cop car but managed to keep my nerve pills. They patted me down, but they never did a full-body search. Daddy and Jannie bailed me out of jail. I snorted my pills in the back seat of their car on the way home. I don't think they saw me; if they did, they didn't say anything.

My poor Momma had to go to the hospital. I was told that she was even put in a neck brace, but I never saw her. She was afraid of me, and I never saw her again in the state of Virginia. This is so hard for me to even talk about, but at the time, I was somewhat numb from all of the drugs. Momma stayed with my ex-stepmom until she could go back to Tennessee. She left Virginia to keep from testifying against me in court. Although my mom wouldn't press charges, the State picked up the case and went forward with the prosecution.

I went to court. The man who called the police was there to testify against me, but since Momma was not there, there was not really a trial. I had a court-appointed lawyer who worked out a deal in which I was given a year of good-behavior probation. The stipulation was that, as long as I didn't get into more trouble, the charges would be dropped.

Around the same time all my court stuff was finalized, Brian and I split up. I soon found a local drug dealer who was the same age as my mom. I moved in with him so that I would have access to drugs. It's not something I'm not proud of at all, but it's the truth. He didn't deal in the hard stuff. He didn't smoke pot or do needles, but he did keep low-grade pain pills at all times. His home was a dry, warm place to lay my head, and I knew I would be fed and could keep a decent buzz, too. I wasn't satisfied, though. I wanted my needle dope. I got some a few times, but it wasn't much. I didn't have the means to get what I really wanted. By then, Momma had also convinced Daddy not to give me more than a few bucks for gas and cigarettes so I wouldn't have enough to get needle dope. I guess they believed that this way, I might not be able to get enough to kill myself or get really strung out; they had tried helping me, and they couldn't do anything with me.

All of this craziness had gone on for a little less than a year. It didn't take me long to make a real mess of everything. I lost almost everything I had in the first two months after Jamie left, but what was left was soon to go, as well. I am not referring to physical possessions only; I lost any bit of myself that I had left.

I wrecked my little green Cavalier several times. I honestly can't even remember how many times I crashed that car. In the first bad wreck, I almost went over the mountain on Red Root Ridge. I was trying to snort cocaine from the dealer in the backseat while driving. Needless to say, that didn't work out very well. Previously, I had snorted plenty of drugs while operating a vehicle, but this time I was so high that I was turned completely around while driving. A tree caught us as we began to slide off the side of the mountain; otherwise, I would likely have been killed or very badly hurt. I was in several other, smaller wrecks, too. My little car was pitiful. The passenger door no longer shut. It was held in by a bungee cord. We got in and out of the passenger side window like the Dukes of Hazzard. After my last wreck in the Cavalier, the insurance company wrote it off as being totaled. I was given some money for the fair market value of the car, but I can't remember how much. All I know is it was enough for me to get high, and I could still drive my car. It was a win-win, or so I thought.

I continued to stay with Sam, the drug dealer, for a while, but my stealing and loss of self-control would soon put that arrangement in jeopardy. I started stealing all kinds of stuff from him. I ripped him off and stole a bunch of his stuff. I don't even remember what all it was, but I had filled my car up with stuff from his house that I was going to take and trade for dope. Steve and Boris, two of Sam's friends, took my car to fix something on it; they did fix the car, but they fixed me, too. They found all of Sam's stuff and gave it back to him. He confronted me. I cried and apologized, and he forgave me and let me keep staying there. Of course, I had to deal with a lot of remarks from his friends, especially his "girlfriends," about me stealing his stuff and using him, but it was the truth, so I really couldn't say anything back. I just kind of blocked them out and acted like I didn't hear them and went on about my business, which was trying to get high by whatever means necessary.

The truth is I was using him, but he was using me too. It was a really messed up situation, but I think he liked it. Having a young girl like me around made him look like the big guy on campus. Here he was with a girl young enough to be his daughter taking care of his house and his kids. It looked like he had it goin' on. I let people think whatever they wanted to think, as long as I had somewhere to sleep, something to eat, and at least enough dope to keep me from going into withdrawals. I hate to admit that I was living that way, but that's how it goes in the drug world at times. Many times, it is even a lot worse.

While I was staying there, I did finally get to start talking to Momma again. I called my Nanny on a regular basis to check in and ask about Momma. She wouldn't tell me anything for a long time except that my mom was okay. Finally, Nanny gave me the number to where Momma was staying in Tennessee. Momma had stayed in Virginia with my ex-stepmom, Gail, for a little while before she moved back home, but she wouldn't have any contact with me at either place for quite some time. Before then, we had never gone any significant period of time without contact. That was really hard on me. I felt awful about myself. Not only had I hurt the person I loved the most in the entire world, the one who had always been there for me no matter what, but she wouldn't even talk to me. She was scared of me and wouldn't have anything to do with me. That is one of the worst feelings I have ever had in my entire life. Then, I moved in with a drug dealer twice my age. Talk about losing all sense of self-worth. I had not only lost self-control but had no sense of self-worth left. It was gone. I was gone. I was slowly checking out, but I wasn't done yet.

As far as Momma was concerned, we were trying to rebuild our relationship during that time. I would call and check on her, and she would call Sam's to make sure I was okay. She was glad I had somewhere to stay and was off of the needle, at least for the most part. She didn't care how old the guy was or that he was a drug dealer; she only cared that I was okay. In spite of everything that had happened, I was still her baby. She still loved me, and I still loved her.

Chapter Twenty-One

Death

I ended up getting kicked out of Sam's house. It was a really bad situation, and it wasn't because of me stealing from him. Actually, it was a lot worse. I guess he really thought that I was his girlfriend, even though I wasn't—or, at least, I didn't know that I was. I was just kind of his live-in. His live-in "what" exactly, I hadn't given much thought to. He had all these other women coming in and out, including two of his ex-wives who came on a regular basis. I was still talking to my last boyfriend, Brian, when I first moved in with Sam. Brian would walk all the way to our trailer park just to see me and talk to me when I first started staying there, but I eventually quit seeing him. Sam would make little jokes about it, but that was the extent of it. I didn't think much about it.

Brian was a little younger than me. Then, I met another guy named Jacob, who was also younger than me. We started hanging out and doing what people on drugs do, but I guess Sam didn't like that too much. To make a long story short, Sam found out that Jacob and I were hanging out in one of the other trailers in his trailer park, so he came up to the trailer, beat Jacob, and that was the end of the story. I got my stuff and left and moved in with Jacob and his family, but I got kicked out of there pretty fast. It didn't last long at all. I don't even really remember what happened. I just remember pulling up to get my hamper full of clothes that had been put outside while I was gone.

Thank God, those days are over. I had absolutely no stability at that time in my life. None whatsoever. No wonder I was such a mess. I had moved around my whole life; I was kind of like a wanderer or a vagabond. I had no roots, no real roots. I didn't have a clue how to be rooted and grounded to even try to stabilize myself. I don't even really remember where I went from there. I honestly can't remember where I lived at that point in time. That says so much about the person that I was during those days. I may have gone back to Sam's after all that mess.

I think maybe I did because I do know that's where I was when I got a phone call that totally rocked my world. I just can't remember for sure if I had been living there ever since I was thrown out of Jacob's place. My life was such a mess, and I was so strung out, but what I do remember about that time is much worse than being a wanderer or a vagabond or anything else I had experienced at that point in my life. With that phone call, I was getting ready to experience something that would change my life forever. I would find out what real hurt and loss felt like. I was getting ready to lose one of the closest people in my life. It was an event that would send my entire family's lives into a tailspin.

My aunt Sissy had been an alcoholic for years. She had dealt with some issues with drugs, too, but her "drug" of choice and number one addiction was alcohol. When she started drinking, however, she would do just about anything else that was around.

The story I put together between the news report, what Nanny was told, what Momma was told, and what some of the people who had been partying with her said afterward, Aunt Sissy had been out drinking and had been high on meth for a few days when she wrecked her car. The accident took Aunt Sissy's life, as well as the life of a close friend of hers who was riding in the car. It happened on Hanging Limb Highway, right outside of Monterey, on Thanksgiving Day in 2003. I never partied with Aunt Sissy a whole lot. I partied with my mom and Uncle Nick, but Aunt Sissy never partied with me much that I can remember. I did know what she liked and how she partied. She liked to do speed like cocaine, crank, or meth to keep her going so she could drink for days at a time.

When Momma called and told me what had happened, I went back to Monterey for the funeral and took Brian with me. I don't remember how he ended up back in the picture, but he rode with me all the way to Monterey, Tennessee, from Richlands, Virginia. It was about a five-hour drive. Of course, I went wasted, so it's a miracle we even made it there in my already-totaled-by-the-insurance-company little green Cavalier. Brian had to climb out of the window of the car when we pulled into my Nanny's yard.

It was the first time I had been there in over a year, but I didn't know any other way except to stay high and blown out of my mind. By that point, it was the only way I knew how to cope. I didn't know how to live day to day without drugs, and I definitely didn't know how to handle anything that hurt me without getting high. I just couldn't deal with reality, so I used drugs to escape as much of it as I could. My answer to everything was to take another Xanax. That's what I had seen almost my whole life, and that's what I did. Momma and Nanny both thought a nerve pill was a cure-all; that's how they dealt with life, and that's how they taught me to deal with life. If I got upset and crying around, they gave me another nerve pill. They really thought they were helping because that's all they knew. They really didn't realize how addicted I was to all drugs, including those nerve pills that they were feeding me like candy to make me "feel better."

Due to all the pills, I can barely remember Aunt Sissy's funeral. I was in really bad shape. I don't remember much about the service or the burial at all. I don't know if it was shock or the drugs or a combination. I would say it was a combination because, as soon as I went up to the casket, I fainted and passed out on the floor. My uncle Nick caught me and took me to the front row of seats until I was able to get myself together. I don't really remember anything about the funeral after that. As I'm sure you can predict, if you have read this much of my story, I did not deal with Aunt Sissy's death very well.

I didn't deal very well with anything that was even somewhat traumatizing, and death was very traumatizing to me for some reason. Loss of any kind was very traumatizing to me. I wasn't one of those people who fainted every time something happened. This was actually the first time I had ever fainted in my life. I had passed out one time from what we thought was low blood sugar (I hadn't eaten), but I had never fainted. I think it was just too much for me to handle. Aunt Sissy was more like my big sister than my aunt (We were about twelve years apart in age). I grew up with my mom, Nanny, Aunt Sissy, and Uncle Nick. That was my family (I didn't have any full-brothers and sisters that I grew up with. I only had half-brothers and sisters and did not really get to know them until after I was an adult). As dysfunctional as my mom's family was, we were all really close. Aunt Sissy's death was probably the hardest hit I had experienced in my life at that time. At least as an adult, I know it was.

So, I did the only thing that I knew how to do: I got high and tried to forget about it. I took comfort in that one true love of mine, crystal meth. I stayed up on meth and pills the entire time I was in Monterey. I just completely numbed out. I found some meth as soon as I got into town (it took all of maybe ten minutes to find it). I literally walked across the road from Nanny's to the apartments where Momma and I used to live to get the dope and stay high, and I didn't lay it down the whole time I was there.

I had been away from Monterey for about two years altogether. I had visited several times, but I didn't do any meth during the visits. I had done a little in Virginia, but it wasn't anything like the stuff I was used to doing back home in Tennessee. That's why I stuck mainly with my pills in Virginia. When I went home for Aunt Sissy's funeral, however, I got ahold of the good stuff, and I couldn't put it down. I really didn't want to put it down, just to be quite frank. I was hurting and in pain and had finally found my love once again, the one thing that could totally numb me out and put me in another world. So, that's what I did. I went to another world by using until I could run like I always did and then headed back to Virginia.

I know some people won't understand this. They will think, *Why wouldn't you straighten up after you saw someone you love die from substance abuse?* I know. It doesn't make any sense, but addiction just doesn't work that way. Yes, sometimes, something like a loved one's death does allow an addict to hit bottom and trigger an awakening of sorts. Most of the time, however, the exact opposite happens. This is because it's the only way we know how to cope with life—use dope, use more dope, and use more powerful dope. My subconscious motto was, "When you start to feel, use more." That's the gist of it. I just wanted to numb out, to numb completely out, because if I had to feel, then I had to deal. I did not know how to deal, so I kept myself numb so I didn't have to feel.

When the funeral was over, I ended my meth escapade and went back to Virginia for more pills. Momma stayed in Tennessee. She moved into Sissy's old apartment and took care of Daisy, Aunt Sissy's daughter. Daisy was just three years old when Aunt Sissy died. One of the saddest things to me right now is that I don't even remember seeing Daisy the whole time I was in Monterey. If Momma had her, I'm sure I did see her, but I can't remember. That breaks my heart because I miss her so much, and I absolutely hate that I couldn't be there for her then. The sad truth is that I couldn't be there for myself, much less anyone else.

The Department of Children Services (DCS) had already been involved in Aunt Sissy and Daisy's lives before Sissy passed away. I think it had something to do with all the "traffic" at Aunt Sissy's apartment, but there may have been more to it. I can't remember the details. What I do know is that Daisy had never been removed from the home before Aunt Sissy passed away. There had been an investigation because Aunt Sissy had gotten in pretty bad shape before she passed—a lot worse than what I realized at the time. Somehow, she did manage to keep a job, but she struggled to take care of Daisy. Aunt Sissy loved Daisy and took care of her when she was straight, but once she started drinking, that was another story.

I watched my aunt spiral out of control after Daisy was born. Most people think having a child would make you want to straighten up, but that is not necessarily the case. Addiction isn't something that always makes sense, especially to someone who has never been addicted. I know that Aunt Sissy loved her little girl and that she wanted to be a good mom because she completely quit drinking and doing any kind of drugs while she was pregnant. It was the happiest I may have ever seen her in my whole life. She was so happy and cheerful. She was tickled to be pregnant. That is some of the best memories I have of her because she was so happy then. She was able to stay straight and wasn't drowning in depression; it was the most joyous I had ever seen her. She thought Daisy was the cutest little thing ever and would laugh and smile over every little thing she did. It was a really big deal for Aunt Sissy to quit partying completely and immediately when she found out she was pregnant.

Aunt Sissy had partied her whole life, ever since she was a teenager, but something changed in her after she had Daisy. I believe she had postpartum depression. I never talked to her about it, but Momma talked to me about it because, when Aunt Sissy came home from the hospital, she would hardly have anything to do with the baby. She seemed to be really withdrawn. She had all the signs of postpartum depression, including not bonding well with the baby. From what I have read about postpartum depression since then, Aunt Sissy had several things going on that may have triggered it—the absence of the baby's father, a family history of depression, and a cesarean section.

Aunt Sissy had also had an abortion several years before and had a nervous breakdown and had to be hospitalized. That was also when her addiction spun out of control, and she had multiple DUI's. After the hospitalization, she was able to get a new job and get her life back on track. She drank and partied some but not bad until after she had Daisy. From a psychological and counseling perspective, it really makes me think this was what caused her to dive back into alcohol. I personally believe that having Daisy reminded her of the abortion, and it was too much for her to handle. The time of the abortion and the period after having Daisy were the only two times I ever saw Aunt Sissy completely out of control. Like I said, she drank and partied, but she was able to maintain and keep her life in order for the most part, other than those two times.

I don't really remember exactly how long it took Aunt Sissy to start drinking again after Daisy was born. I know it wasn't immediately. She made a really serious attempt at staying straight and being a normal mom. Momma and Nanny helped her a lot because of the surgery, and I know she didn't drink during that time. She really tried, but for some reason, she wasn't able to stay away from it. In time, Aunt Sissy's addiction to alcohol cost her her life.

Momma kept Daisy when Sissy passed away, but that did not last long. DCS had to take Daisy away from Momma due to Momma's drug use. Momma was devastated and was determined to get Daisy back. She got a lawyer and went to rehab to get help with her addiction. She even went to outpatient and recovery meetings after she got out of rehab. She was committed to getting Daisy back. She loved that little girl so much! She loved her like her own. Momma and Nanny had pretty much raised Daisy while Sissy was working and partying, so they were both devastated when DCS stepped in.

When I found out what was going on, I decided to go back to Tennessee and help Momma. I know now that this was a really bad idea, but, at the time, somehow, I didn't get that. I still don't really know what kind of help I thought I could be, but that was supposedly the plan. Truthfully, I think I just wanted to go back to my family. I missed my momma so much and wanted to be there with her, especially after my aunt had passed away. This was a really hard time for all of us. Even though I was an adult, I remember lying on Momma and crying like a baby because I missed Aunt Sissy so much. When I did get back to Tennessee, it all became very real to me. We were living in Aunt Sissy's apartment, but she was gone. It didn't matter how many drugs I did, I couldn't totally numb that out or get away from that anymore. It was right in my face, and I couldn't completely escape from it anymore.

Before I went back to Monterey, I was halfway straight—according to my definition of straight back then, that is. I had gotten off of the needle again for the most part. I just used it every once in a while and was just doing some pills and smoking weed. I believe I really thought I was in good shape and could help, and I guess, for me at that time, I was doing fairly well.

Sometime after Sissy's passing, I had lost my car. It had broken down on the four-lane in front of the Cedar Bluff, VA overlook park, and I left it parked there. I didn't have the money to get it towed, so I had no other choice. The first night it was parked there, someone busted out one of my windows and stole my CD player. The next day, someone busted the windshield and every other window out of it. My dad and Jannie thought it was probably just young people vandalizing, but I figured it was someone I had ripped off during one of my drug-fueled stealing sprees. I had seen several vehicles sit in the exact same place for longer periods of time and never get touched, but I accepted that I deserved that one.

Daddy ended up getting somebody to tow it for me. The guy offered me $100 for the parts and metal. So, of course, I took it. I wasn't about to tell my daddy because I thought I had to have that money to get high. Daddy and Jannie knew I was planning on going back to Tennessee to help Momma with Daisy's situation, so they bought me a car from her sister's husband so I could drive to Tennessee and get a job. I did eventually do that, but it didn't last long.

I still don't fully understand my reasoning or how I could be of help to anyone back home. I guess that it just shows how the addicted brain works. It's very foggy and does not make much sense to anyone who is not using. I barely remember going to Jannie's sister's house to pick up the car; I couldn't get back there today if I had to. I slept in the back seat of Daddy's vehicle almost all the way there. I'm not even sure how I even managed to drive the car away from the lady's house. Maybe that nap helped, I don't know, but, anyway, that was the plan: me, on the road, back to Tennessee.

Chapter Twenty-Two

Close Call

When I got back to Monterey, I moved in with Momma at Aunt Sissy's old apartment. I partied on pot and pills with Momma and some of her friends when I first got back, but it didn't take me long to get back to the hard stuff. I got up with my best friend, Lori, and that was all she wrote, as the old saying goes. Lori had gotten strung out on crack really bad while I was in Virginia, so that's what we ended up doing pretty much every day. Not only had Lori gone wild, but she had also become really good friends with one of the biggest cocaine dealers in town.

Lori and the dealer would come to Momma's apartment, and we would all get smoked up. We would cook the cocaine up into crack, smoke it, and stay blown away for days. We thought it was a safe place to be able to party and stay off of the roads, but I was bad to mix pills with the crack. I was still hooked on pills pretty badly and wasn't able to lay them down yet. The crack just wasn't enough for me, not like it once was back in the day. I needed the pills, too, and I wanted all I could get. Simply put, I wanted to get as high as I could possibly get and stay that way as long as I possibly could. At one time, I liked to just get really high and buzzing, but the further I went into addiction, the more I wanted to be completely blown away to the point where I didn't know what was even going on. That became my goal. Aunt Sissy's passing and us living in her old apartment (I stayed in Daisy's old room) just made things worse. It made me want to check out even that much more, and that is just about what I did.

One night we were all sitting in my room smoking dope. The dealer kept telling us to take a break, but I wouldn't. I just kept asking for more, cooking up more, and smoking more. I was also snorting Percocet (oxycodone, an opioid narcotic) in between hitting the pipe. Lori had been urging me to quit using the pills while we were smoking. It scared her, but I wouldn't stop. I couldn't stop. I just kept going with it and using as much as I could until, finally, I overdid it. They both kept trying to warn me, but I wouldn't listen. I just kept going and going and going until the inevitable happened.

The last thing I remember, I was sitting on the end of the bed and hitting the pipe. My body started to draw up to my right side. I still had the pipe and was still hitting it, but I was fading fast. The next thing I remember was going out, and I felt myself hit the boxes on the floor (I still hadn't unpacked my stuff from Virginia because I was too busy partying). By this time, I was completely passed out. I don't know what happened after I hit the boxes because I blacked out. The next thing I remember, I was on the hallway floor with my shirt off. I was soaking wet.

The others who were there with me told me that my body turned gray, my lips turned purple, and they couldn't get a pulse. They really thought I was going to die—or was already dead, which I may have been. I'm not really sure. I just know I was out. Out. Momma started to pray, and Lori laid hands on me and started to pray, too, because they thought I was really gone. That's when I came to and regained consciousness. I'm not sure what exactly Lori prayed, but I will never forget my momma's prayer.

I didn't hear it at the time, of course, but she told me about it later. She told me that she asked God to save me even if it meant that He had to take her instead of me. She told Him that she had lived a good life. She had the chance to be married and have a child, but I had never experienced anything like that. All I had ever known was the drug world. I didn't know what life was really about.

Callous as it sounds now, I didn't think much about Momma's prayer at the time. I also didn't care much that I had almost died (or maybe even was dead for a few minutes, I don't really know). As I regained consciousness, I started freaking out because they had taken off my shirt in front of the dealer. Then, I got really upset because the dealer himself was freaking out because of what had happened to me. Once I had crept back from the abyss of the overdose, the main point of contention was that I wanted more drugs, and they wouldn't give me anymore. I did finally talk Momma into giving me a muscle relaxer and a little weed, so I could go to sleep. Lori was really scared. She was so worried about me. We had been best friends since we were ten, but we were more like sisters. She stayed for a while to make sure I was going to be alright. When I got ready to go to sleep, and she knew I was okay, she finally left.

Momma made me sleep in her bed that night. She wanted to be right there with me to make sure I was okay. Even though all I was worried about was getting high again, I do remember feeling weak that night and having a fleeting thought that I might go to sleep and not wake up. I felt a little fear, but it was just for a minute. The feeling passed quickly.

I'm pretty sure I was the only one who didn't think it was a big deal to go into convulsions and almost die. To be honest, I don't think I really cared whether I lived or died at that time anyway. I didn't have anything to live for except to get high, and that feeling of being in another world that came with the drugs went away all too quickly. Most people would think an overdose would be a wake-up call, but it wasn't, at least not for me. To tell you the truth, I didn't even think much about it back then. It was, at most, a temporary blip on the radar screen of someone who was otherwise completely consumed with the business of being a full-time drug addict. All I could think about was that I wanted to get high and that I *needed* to get high. That had been my whole life for so long; a "little thing" like it almost killing me was no comparison to the pull that the addiction had on me (I know. *I know*. It sounds absolutely crazy, but you have to remember that drug addiction is both mental and physical. An addict needs the drugs, not just to cope but, sometimes, even to live. The drugs can get such a strong hold on the body and the mind that an abrupt stop can be physically harmful—potentially even fatal—especially with alcohol and opiates).

• • •

The night of my overdose, Momma told me that there would be no more smoking dope at her place. The dealer was scared, too, and so was Lori. That "putting her foot down" mentality didn't last long. It is all kind of fuzzy now, but, if I remember right, we were smoking the very next day. We did go out to a hotel to smoke a few times, but eventually, we were right back at Momma's. She even joined in. With her personal addiction being what it was, she couldn't say no, not with it right in her face like that. I wonder now whether she got so lost in the drugs that she forgot about her prayer to God.

The whole crack thing kind of faded away after a while. I wanted my true drug of choice, and that was not crack cocaine. Also happening in the background during this time: the dealer had started running with different people, and Lori took spells where she would try to straighten up. She would take a few days to recuperate and try to get herself together, but that stuff was not for me. I couldn't take days off. I never was like that. Addiction was my life, all day, every day. That's all I knew, and that's all I wanted. I was getting ready to get my true love back once again.

It began when Momma had a guy named Joe come over with some dope. Joe had been a friend of my aunt Sissy. He was a wild-looking guy. He looked like he had come straight out of the woods, for real. He didn't cut his hair or his beard, which was bushy and curly and white—almost solid white. He was the kind of fellow who would probably scare you if you didn't know him, but when you became acquainted, he was such a sweet, nice guy. I think he had actually been diagnosed as being schizophrenic; he heard things and talked to himself. Honestly, I am not sure whether he had always been that way or whether his prolonged use of crystal meth had made him that way. Meth was his drug of choice, and he never went without it. He made sure that he had it every single day.

The day that I met Joe at the apartment was the first time that my mom and I had done meth together in years. Momma and Joe had been in her room for a while, and she kept telling me that she would have him bring me some in the other room. We had smoked just a little bit together in the kitchen before they went into the bedroom. It was just enough to get me started. Once I got started, I couldn't stop. I couldn't handle them being in the other room using and me sitting out there by myself without any dope. I just wasn't having it. I wouldn't leave them alone. I went to Momma's bedroom door, and, finally, she finally let me in. Looking back now, I wish I had never crossed the threshold.

• • •

Walking through that door into Momma's room changed everything. In so many ways, I wish I had never gone to that door at all, and I certainly wish I hadn't walked through it to the other side. This is really hard for me to talk about because the reason that Momma had me locked out was that she and Joe were in the bedroom shooting up. My precious (but very flawed) mother, who had begged God to save my life, even if it meant that He would take hers, had turned to the needle. This was the first time I had ever seen Momma using a needle to get high. Before that day, I had never even known of her shooting up, much less seen it firsthand. That day also marked the first time that Momma ever saw me shoot up. Clearly, a line had been crossed, and we would never be able to go back to the other side.

My mother was not naïve; she knew I had shot up with meth and other drugs in the past—not just a little, but a lot. She had found my needles, and she had seen the marks on my arms. Still, she had never allowed me to do it in her presence. That was the one thing that she forbade, and she wouldn't budge on it. At least, she had never budged before that day. Looking back, it's like a little part of me died that day, and the way that I viewed Momma forever changed. I know now that she had probably been doing it for years, but actually seeing her with that needle in her arm for the first time altered the way that I saw her. It definitely wasn't a change for the better. There was absolutely nothing inside of me that thought, *This is good. Momma is cool now. I won't have to hide anymore*. It was quite the contrary, actually. I know this probably sounds hypocritical, but I never liked the idea of Momma shooting up. I didn't like to think about it, and I certainly did not like to see it.

A part of me was shocked and surprised to see *my momma* shooting up that day. I never thought she would go there, partly because she was always so hard on me for doing it. She always seemed so disappointed in me for resorting to that measure of using (Maybe, just maybe, that was because she herself understood where that road would lead). Looking back, I see now that her addiction had progressed much more than I realized while I had been living in Virginia. I think she may have been using the needle for quite a while before I came back to Tennessee. She was probably shooting cocaine when she and a previous boyfriend would go in the other room while the rest of us were smoking in the bedroom. I just didn't put two and two together until I saw it with my own eyes.

Even though she was the mother and I was the child, somehow, I blamed myself. I see now how codependent our relationship was, but, back then, I blamed myself for her going back to Tennessee after our fight in Virginia. I also blamed myself for my own shooting up all those years, which I thought made Momma think it wasn't that big of a deal. Now that I am at a different place in my life, I know that it is unhealthy and self-destructive to dwell on those thoughts. My mom was a grown woman. She was supposed to be the adult and the parent in our relationship. It just didn't always work that way (I understand now that Nanny had not been much of an example to Momma of proper parenting, and, of course, neither had Grandpa Oden. However, none of that was my fault, as I was not even born yet).

Soon after that horrific day when Momma and I shot up in front of one another for the first time, Momma tried to get help for her drug addiction. It was not so much for herself but, rather, to increase her chances of regaining custody of Aunt Sissy's little girl, Daisy. Momma went to a drug rehabilitation treatment center, planning to straighten herself up so she could get Daisy. Bless her heart; I did not make things any easier for her. Nevertheless, she did at least part of what she set out to do.

Momma went through inpatient treatment at a drug rehabilitation center called Bradford. While she was there, it was mandatory that she attend recovery meetings. These are meetings for people who have had (or who still have) a drug problem. Those who attend these meetings support one another through their recovery in hopes they can stay clean themselves. The treatment center also told Momma to go continue to meetings when she was released, and she did.

Bradford had an outpatient center in Crossville, a town about half an hour from Monterey. There, they had meetings that were open to the public. Momma went to those a few times a week. A bus came to our apartment, picked her up, and brought her back home after the meetings. She even went to a few Alcoholics Anonymous ("AA") meetings there in Monterey, but she didn't like them. I went with her once to an AA meeting in Monterey. She tried to encourage me to go with her to Crossville. She said she thought I would really like it and could relate to the younger crowd. She would tell me about all the kids there my age, drinking coffee and smoking cigarettes, but I was not the least bit interested. The only thing I was interested in was getting high. Straightening my life out was the furthest thing from my mind at that time. Now, of course, I wish that I would have gone with Momma to her meetings. Maybe we could have straightened up together and finally made it out of that dysfunctional, chaotic mess that we were living in, but that's not what happened. There is nothing that I can do to change that path now.

As far as Momma was concerned, she managed to stay off all the street drugs like crystal meth, cocaine, and pot, but she still took her prescription pills. She was prescribed Lortab pain pills and sometimes Percocet pain pills due to her physical disability from the wreck that occurred years earlier. She had a lot of pain due to the damage to her collar bone and the loss of a majority of the use in her right hand. She also took two types of nerve pills, Xanax and Klonopin, for bipolar disorder and anxiety. She was prescribed lots of other medicines for each of those conditions, as well, but those were the only narcotics she was prescribed at that time. Well, she did get Neurontin, which is for nerve pain, seizures, and, sometimes, for bipolar disorder (which she had been diagnosed with), but it wasn't a narcotic back then. It is now.

I remember my mom getting mad because someone from the meetings told her she needed to come off of the prescription medicine, too. They told her that those medications were considered drugs, too, just like all the other stuff she had been using. Momma had never abused pills much before. She didn't even normally take as many as they prescribed her. She really couldn't with me around because I got most of them. I understand now that the people at the meetings were right. Once she got off of all the other stuff, she started abusing pills, especially pain pills. She substituted. Most of the time, if someone who is addicted cannot, or chooses not to, use their drug of choice, they usually substitute with whatever they can use. It's like telling someone on a diet that they can't have the two-layer chocolate cake in the refrigerator but then leaving a plate of warm cookies out on the counter; the "fix" may come in a different package, but it will still come. In Momma's case, prescription drugs were the only thing that she could do and still pass her drug tests to get Daisy back. So, that's what she did—pain pills and plenty of them.

Chapter Twenty-Three

Selfishness

During the time that Momma was trying to get clean so that she could get custody of Daisy, I was doing the polar opposite. I had no intention whatsoever of trying to straighten up myself. I wanted to help Momma with Daisy, but my desire to get high was too strong. I was only twenty-two years old. I had just gotten back to my old stomping grounds, and it was party time for me. When I first went back to Monterey, I did have at least some fear of meth and the needle in general because I had been down that oh-so-rocky road before. After being back in town for a couple of months, however, those fears were long gone. I was no longer concerned about drugs or the needle destroying my life or having control of me anymore; in that short time, my addiction had already progressed to the point where all rational thinking and reasoning were completely gone.

The fear had once protected me, at least to a certain extent. It had kept me away from my old hang-outs, old friends, and old dealers. Once the drugs that I was doing drowned out that fear, I not only went back to the needle and crystal meth, but my addiction progressed to the point where I actually went to even worse places than I had before (oh, yes, that was quite possible) and did worse things than I had before in order to get drugs. That's how addiction works, folks. It progresses in a negative direction, from bad to worse and so on. Even if it's arrested at some point for a period of time, it always resurfaces and gets worse than it was before. The only exceptions are when the addict gets effective treatment or when there is divine intervention.

Obviously, I started going to the same "ole playgrounds," looking for the same "ole playmates," and of course, I started "playing the same ole game." Before long, I was even back into the "cooking game." The majority of my old dealers and old cooks were in the county jail or the state penitentiary by this time, but I managed to get in with the new ones. Before I moved to Virginia, most of the dealers and cooks had been older than me. By the time I moved back to Tennessee, the majority of them were my age or even younger.

A lot of the people who were running the game and cooking the dope when I got back in town weren't even part of the party scene when I left Monterey two years before. The last that I had known about most of them, they were still in high school, maybe drinking some and smoking a little pot, but certainly not on meth or anything hard. It was a small town, and I knew most of the new players, so it wasn't hard to get back into the game. I had grown up with most of those guys. So, there I was, back at it, full-force, once again.

Luke, my old boyfriend, was still around and still in the game. He had spent a little time in jail, but it didn't faze him. He was back at it, as usual. We didn't date this time, but we did run around together and party a little. I actually ended up dating his best friend, Garrison. He was a little younger than me. When I had left Monterey, Garrison was still in high school playing football. While I was away in Virginia, his football career had ended, and his days as a meth cook had begun.

Luke and Garrison had become partners in crime, both literally and figuratively. They had started cooking together and become partners while I was gone, and they made some mean stuff. I'm not trying to glorify the dope or the cooks but, rather, to explain how drugs can be so different from town to town and cook to cook. As I mentioned in an earlier chapter, I had tried a little meth in Virginia, but I was able to walk away from it. It just didn't get ahold of me like Luke and Garrison's did. This was some powerful stuff. I hadn't done any dope like that in years, and I was hooked—instantly! I was already using a myriad of other drugs and was not in the best of shape, but I had found my true love once again—the needle and meth—and I was gone. Addiction had fully taken over. Luke and Garrison both shot up, too, so that made it easier for me. We could all get high together.

They were letting me do shots as big as theirs, and they were pretty big guys. I only weighed a little over one hundred pounds at the time. Luke weighed around 200 pounds. Garrison weighed between 250 and 300 pounds; he had been a big football player. Despite the drug use, he still wasn't a small guy. Street drugs are just like other drugs and alcohol. The larger you are, the more you can take and the more you need to reach a certain level. They broke me in the right this time. When I first started doing shots as big as theirs, it blew me away; it was hard for me to even function. Before long, I needed just as much as they did to even get high.

I happened to be the only one who had a car, so that was my ticket to stay high. Neither of them had a car, nor did the local dealer. Since none of them had a vehicle, they needed me, plus I was dating the head cook. I was back in the game. If they had dope, I had dope because they couldn't get anywhere without me. I'm sure they could have gotten another ride from somebody, but they knew they could trust me as far as the law (police) was concerned. When you're in the game, you try to stick with people you think you can trust, especially on meth because it can make you paranoid and "geek" out on everybody, thinking they are snitches or working for the authorities; so, if you feel you can trust someone, you usually stick pretty tight with them.

We didn't have any elaborate labs. We usually carried a portable lab, which meant we could haul everything in my car. I would take them, along with their lab, and drop them off somewhere to cook, and they would give me a specific time to come back by to get them. I wasn't allowed to come around while they were cooking this time like I had in the past. I would drop them off when no one was around and pick them up when no one was around without anyone knowing of the specific location. This was very different than the way we had done things in the past when we cooked at different peoples' homes. We were less likely to get caught this new way. Sometimes, they would go to abandoned houses to cook or even just go way out in the woods and use a Coleman stove. The fewer people who knew what was going on, the safer we were and the less likely we were to get caught. It had gotten so "hot" in the meth game, it was hard to cook and not get caught, but they had a pretty good system. At least, we thought so at the time. Once a batch was done, we would ditch the lab somewhere until we needed it again.

There were quite a few times that we went to Momma's apartment to party and hang out or just rest from all the running and not sleeping or eating. Momma did not use meth with us this go-around. She was trying to stay straight to get Daisy back, so she didn't party with us. She really didn't even know what was going on. We stayed in the bedroom with the door shut and kept everything hid from her, but she knew the game and knew who I was with and how I was acting, so I'm sure she knew what was happening on some level. She just ignored us most of the time and went on about her business. She would rarely come to the apartment while we were there. She usually stayed at her boyfriend's house or would go to Nanny's. Now looking back, I see this took some enormous willpower and determination on her part. It makes me see even that much more how much she really loved Daisy.

I know that was so disrespectful of me to bring all of that mess around Momma when she was trying to get clean so that she could get Daisy, but drugs have no respect for anyone or anything, and neither do the people using the drugs. One time, I even let Momma drive my car to Nanny's with a meth lab in the trunk. I knew that if I told her that the lab was in there, she would have run us off and made us leave the apartment. That was so selfish and awful of me! I still can't believe I did that, but that's what drugs do to you: they make you forget about, or at least not care about, anyone or anything except your next high.

Lots of times, we would bring our duffle bag containing our supplies into the apartment. We would walk up the sidewalk in broad daylight like nothing was going on, like we were just carrying our clothes around. I guess we thought the neighbors would just think my friend was there for an overnight visit. We even cooked on the Coleman stove at least once in Daisy's old room. I don't remember why they weren't able to finish in the woods that time. I think they were running late when I got there, or maybe they got spooked. I can't remember for sure. Either way, even though the more dangerous part of the process had been done somewhere else, this was still very stupid and careless on my part. We could have all gotten busted in Momma's apartment and gone to jail for a very long time, Momma included.

I definitely wasn't helping Momma get Daisy back in any way whatsoever. If anything, I was diminishing any and all chances of that ever happening. Things finally got so bad that Momma wouldn't even stay at the apartment when we were there. I suppose she was afraid we would get caught, and she would be dragged into it with us. In her mind, she probably thought that, as long as she wasn't there, she couldn't be charged if we got busted, and she could still get Daisy. In reality, the place was rented in her name, and she probably would have gotten in almost as much trouble as us, if not more, and she definitely would have lost any chance of getting custody of Daisy.

By the grace of God, we never got busted with a lab on us, but there was one time when we ditched a bag, and our supplies were found. I freaked out, thinking that the police would use our fingerprints to bust us. One of Momma's pill bottles was even in the bag. I had used it to store something and had been too stupid and too high to peel the label with her name off the bottle. If the cops were watching us, they must have known that she wasn't involved this time and was just an innocent bystander because she didn't get in any trouble, despite my stupidity.

As far as I know, no one was ever questioned about the bag of supplies. I'm not sure if there wasn't enough evidence, or maybe they just decided to watch and try to get us for more than whatever relatively minor charge the supply bust would have yielded. I suspect that it was the latter because, one night after that, Garrison and I were in Crossville, and the cops got after us. He was driving my car, and we were on our way to his mom's house that night. We didn't have a lab, any supplies, or anything like that in the car, but of course, the police didn't know that. All we had were our syringes full of dope, a couple of scrap baggies for "hard times," and some rolling papers. When the cops got behind us and turned on the blue lights, Garrison told me to throw the stuff out the window. He then tried to outrun the officer and get us to his mom's house.

I must have thought he was going to be able to get away from the cop, or maybe I really just couldn't let go of my dope. I refused to throw it out. I just couldn't let it go. I put it under the seat, where, of course, the cops found it after we were stopped. We were both taken to jail and charged with resisting arrest and possession of drug paraphernalia. Thank God we were not charged with the dope in the needles. Tennessee is extremely hard on meth crimes. I don't know why they didn't charge us with the meth that was in the needles or the scrape baggies (meth tends to stick to the bag, the bag is then used to scrape and get high again even when it doesn't look like there is anything there—hence, the name "scrape" baggies). Maybe they thought it was too much trouble to send it to the lab and only be able to charge us with simple possession.

Garrison ended up doing sixty days in jail. He was already on probation in that county, so he went ahead and flattened his time for probation. I spent fourteen hours in the holding cell before Momma could get the money wired from Daddy to get me out. I passed out while I was in the holding cell. When I came to, one of the lady officers was standing over me, freaking out. I had been out for about twelve hours, and they had been trying to get me up for the last hour. She already had the nurse on the way to check on me, but I was fine. I had just crashed because I had been up so long. I don't remember how long I had been up. I would stay up for days on meth, sometimes weeks.

If you are reading this and you have never been a drug user yourself, you may be thinking that I would have hit rock bottom at this point. Unfortunately, that is not true…not by a long shot. When I was released, I took a turn for the worse and began using some of my old tricks to get dope. My supply guy was in jail, and his partner wasn't much use to me without him. He really didn't have the means to keep the ball rolling. I traded Garrison's Play Station 2 to one of his friends for meth while he was in jail. I also engaged in lots of other crazy drug-using and drug-getting behavior—very shameful activity that I won't go into in detail about. You can use your imagination, and sadly most of what comes to mind, if not all, would be true.

Right before I went to jail, I had started running around out in a small neighboring town, Clarkrange. (You may remember me mentioning "Crankrange" earlier; it was where Uncle Nick had been when he came to Nanny's high as a kite, geeking out that morning that middle-school me was trying to get ready for school). Someone always had dope out that way. I even took Luke out there with me a few times. That was a big mistake.

I stole one of the ingredients that was needed to make meth from Luke and took it out there. Then, I did the same to one of the guys out there, Bear, and took it back to Monterey. I stole the other dealer's walkie-talkies. Soon, I had double-crossed pretty much every one of my connections. Somehow, they all managed to forgive me and let it go, or so I thought anyway. Bear ended up holding me at gunpoint and making me take him to look for the stuff that I had taken. I'm pretty sure he knew what had really happened because of the way he treated me after that, but he never stopped filling me full of dope. I actually ended up living with him off and on for a while. Crazy, I know! But, again, this is a somewhat "normal" life in the drug world, especially in the meth world, and it had become normal to me. Somehow, it seems perfectly rational to cohabitate with someone who has held you at gunpoint (in my case) or who has habitually stolen from you and is just using you to get dope (in his case). That's just how it rolls in that "world."

When Garrison got out of jail, we got back together and stayed at my Nanny's for a little while. He never got back into the cooking scene in the same way that he had been before he went to jail. I think he and Luke had a hard time coming up with all the supplies again. It was difficult to come up with the money and the means to start a completely new lab back then. This was way before the shake-and-bake method (a simplified but much more dangerous way to make meth) that is used by some cooks today. This was back in 2004. The cooking process not only took a long time but required a lot of ingredients and cooking utensils.

Before I moved back in with the other guy from Clarkrange (Bear), Garrison went with me to court. He had already pled guilty to the drug charges, so he went with me to make sure they dropped the charge against me. In our minds, there wasn't any reason for both of us to pay for that particular crime (even though I was the stupid one who refused to throw the dope out the window, he was still willing to take the blame). The district attorney agreed to drop the drug charge and only charge me with resisting arrest. I was given probation. Garrison and I left the courthouse, and I don't really remember much about him after that.

It makes me feel incredibly bad to remember the way that I used people and all of the terrible things that I did to get drugs. It's really hard to be honest about these things, but I feel that God wants me to be truthful so that those out who are still living this way (or have lived this way or have a loved one who's living this way) can know that they are not alone and understand how drugs really change you, how you become another person, how you lose yourself in the process. I was there, but I'm not there anymore. Thank God I am not the person I once was. I have tried to clean up this account of my life during those horrible years as much as possible to keep it from being too graphic. Believe it or not, I have only mentioned a few representative high points (or, more accurately, low points) so that readers can get an idea of what my life as a drug addict was like without me delving into every wretched detail of that time period. Still, this has all been very hard to talk about openly and honestly. I have to remind myself, even now, that I am a new creation in Christ and that all things have passed away (1 Corinthians 5:17). Thank God that old girl is dead!

Chapter Twenty-Four

Bottom

Somewhere in the mix of all the chaos going on in my life, in 2004, Momma found out she that was not going to be able to get Daisy. Her attorney said that it was because she was disabled, was unmarried, didn't have enough income, and was physically unable to care for a small child. Momma was absolutely devastated—and furious. If these were the reasons why she couldn't get custody of Daisy, Momma thought that, surely, the lawyer had known this all along. None of these "issues" were new developments. She felt that the lawyer just took her money, knowing that she would never win the case and that she had gone through rehab and tried to stay straight for nothing.

Up until this time, we had been visiting Daisy regularly. We went to the Department of Children Services for the visits at first. Nanny, Momma, and I usually went together. Momma never missed a visit, but Nanny and I missed a few. Nanny was sick, and I was an addict. Unlike me, Momma could keep it together enough to go see Daisy even when she was using.

My uncle Nick wasn't allowed to see Daisy at all because of his felony drug charge. He had spent nine months in jail after getting busted with a meth lab in the trunk of his car and was then sent to a halfway house (a sober-living facility) at the time. The lab wasn't his, but he went to jail instead of getting the other guy in trouble, out of loyalty, possibly partly because the owner was a big player in the meth world and had to be protected in order to keep supplies rolling and maybe even more likely because this same guy had saved my uncle Nick's life while swimming at a river when he was just a teenager. They were all drinking years before meth use. My uncle had dove in. The now "cook" was the only one who noticed that my uncle never came back up. He dove in and saved him.

The guys staying in the halfway house where Uncle Nick stayed had to stay straight, hold down a job, pay rent, do chores, pass drug tests, and attend the recommended number of meetings. With a good support system finally there to back him up, Uncle Nick actually did really well there and was no longer using drugs. After a period of time, he was even trusted to supervise the other males in the home, but he was still never allowed to see Daisy.

After Momma, Nanny, and I had several visits with Daisy at the DCS office, we were allowed to see her at McDonald's. There was a playground there where Daisy and I would play while the others talked to Momma about how Daisy was doing with her new family. The visit I remember most vividly took place after Momma knew she wasn't going to get custody, but Daisy's foster mom allowed us to see her again anyway. Momma just sat and cried the whole time while Daisy and I played. Daisy's soon-to-be new mom saw how much Momma loved Daisy, so she agreed to let us continue to see her. The adoptive mom and her husband were wonderful Christian people. I see now how God was protecting Daisy, not only from the drug life my family was living and had lived but, even more so, from what was soon to happen. However, it wasn't easy at the time for Momma or me.

I never saw Daisy again after that visit, but I'm pretty sure Momma did. For me, it was easier to handle if I acted like it wasn't happening. That's pretty much how I dealt with everything at that time in my life: *out of sight, out of mind.* Now, I wish I had made an effort to see her, but, at the time, I just couldn't handle it. So, I did what I did best back then, which was to run away and get high. I believe it was harder on Momma than it was on anyone. Daisy was more like a little sister to me than a cousin, but she was more like a daughter to my mom than a niece. My mom had now lost not only her younger sister, whom she helped raise and who looked to Momma very much as a mother figure, but now she had lost Daisy, too.

Not surprisingly, this is when Momma took a turn for the worse. I don't think she could handle reality anymore. She quickly got in really bad shape, the worst I had ever seen her, even worse than when I was in high school and we lost our apartment. This was a different kind of worse. Is there a word for worse than worse? If there is, that's what she was. After she lost the apartment that had been Aunt Sissy's, she moved in with Lee, a male friend of hers. I don't know that they ever actually "dated," but he did take care of her financially. He didn't drink alcohol or use drugs, but he was disabled and got lots of pain pills from the doctor. Whatever pills we didn't use, Lee sold in order to get money for other things. Between the money and the pills, he enabled Momma and helped her keep her habit up. He was also a diabetic on insulin and had plenty of syringes. He kept us both in stock with clean needles. Before long, Momma was back to shooting coke (cocaine).

One of my worst visual memories is of my mom sitting on Lee's bathroom floor, shooting cocaine into her breasts and stomach. I was shooting the drugs with her, as well. Even high on cocaine and other drugs, I promise you that is not something you ever want to see: your mother shooting dope in her breasts and stomach. It's an awful visual image and a memory that I wish I could totally forget. I do not share this to degrade my mother in any way. I knew my mom, and I knew her heart, and I truly believe she would want others to know these things if it could keep them from having the same end as hers was soon to be.

I didn't shoot coke with Momma much after seeing her do that. I just couldn't. Besides, I had already slowed way down on cocaine and crack after I had overdosed on crack (Crack is just a cooked form of cocaine). I used crack quite a bit right after the overdose (and had been using cocaine off and on for years), but after some time, my body began to react differently to crack and cocaine. It was kind of scary, enough so that I mostly stayed off of it and favored other drugs from that point on.

The last time I remember smoking crack, I had been up for a few days on meth and was in the process of coming down. The dealer gave me a pretty good-sized hit of crack. I remember him saying, "Give Cherie a good one. She likes this stuff" (as I explained earlier, Cherie is my middle name and what I went by back home in Tennessee). I had known this dealer for a long time; my boyfriend and I had started smoking crack with him way back when I was a young teenager. That hit that he gave me hit me hard and laid me back. After I handed the pipe back, I just laid on the bed and didn't move or speak for a long time. I couldn't do either. It basically paralyzed me.

The very last time I ever shot coke was with Momma. She gave me a shot the size that she was used to doing, and I wasn't used to coke much by then. I did the big shot she gave me and went numb from head to toe. I managed to make it to the couch in the living room. I couldn't feel my face or any part of my body. I couldn't move. I couldn't speak. The crack overdose I had experienced the year before must have done something to me because coke had never affected me like that in the past. I had done coke since I was about thirteen years old, and I was twenty-three at this time (and twenty-two when I overdosed on crack).

After the overdose, any time that I ran out of meth and began to go through withdrawals, my eyes would roll up in my head, and I couldn't get them to go down. I couldn't look down or focus. I believe the overdose had done something to my brain and was causing seizures. I had gone through withdrawals plenty of times before, but I had never had any problems like that. I'm pretty sure I was having small seizures, but if I could get some nerve pills, Neurontin, or dope, they would stop. Nerve pills and Neurontin are both used to treat seizures; dope would make the withdrawals stop. I tried pot, too, but it didn't work the same. It would calm me down and chill me out some, but I had to have it on top of the dope, nerve pills, or Neurontin for it to really help. The mild seizures from withdrawal were pretty freaky, but they didn't stop me—or even slow me down.

Now, I was in bad shape, Momma was in bad shape, and we had lost Daisy. Things were not looking good for us. Momma wanted me to go back to Virginia before I died or went to jail for a long time, but I was tied to Tennessee by law through probation. Daddy and Jannie had agreed for me to go back and stay with them in Virginia, but I had to go to my probation officer and ask for a transfer. She said she would have everything ready at our next visit.

I knew she would drug test me before she would transfer me. I did quit smoking pot because I knew it would take a long time to get out of my system (I had learned that lesson as a juvenile while on probation). I continued to use meth until a week or so before the drug test because I knew that it wouldn't take as long to clear my system. I stayed with

Momma the week before my visit to keep from using other drugs, but that didn't work out so well. I talked her into giving me some pain pills and nerve pills because I just couldn't do it. I couldn't stay sober. I couldn't make it without some kind of drugs in my system. I hoped by some miracle they would be out of my system or that the probation officer wouldn't test me. Wrong! I failed my drug test due to the presence of both opiates and benzos in my system (Benzodiazepines are a class of psychoactive drugs that are used to treat anxiety and help control seizures; they include Lorazepan, Diazepam, and several others).

Failing my drug test meant that I had violated the conditions of my probation, and I had to go back to court. Momma and Lee took me to court on October 4, 2004. They waited in the car while I went up to the courtroom. Several of us were taken into a room across the hall from the courtroom, along with our court-appointed lawyers. The probation officers came over to the room, talked to the lawyers, and told them what our sentences would be. Then, we were supposed to go back across the hall to be formally sentenced by the judge. I was told that I would have to spend thirty days in jail.

When it was my turn to go across the hall and be sentenced, I hightailed it out of there as fast as I could go. I walked as fast as I could out of that courthouse without running and looking obvious, got into Lee's car, laid down in the back seat, and told Lee, "Go!" I couldn't go thirty days without dope! In my mind, there was no way that I could possibly do that. Momma tried to talk me into going back up to the courtroom, but there was no way I was going to jail. I kept telling Lee to drive us away from the courthouse, and Momma finally gave in and said it was okay, so we left. Now, I was officially "on the run" for the first time in my life.

I stayed with Bear (the guy I had lived with before in another county) most of the time after that. I never thought the cops would look for me there, and they didn't. I did stay with Momma and Lee a few times but not much. I was afraid I would get caught there and go to jail.

Momma would have Lee bring her to Bear's to see me when she hadn't seen me in a few days, but she never came inside. They would pull into the driveway, make sure I was okay, give me some pot and pills, and leave. I never thought one of those random check-in-and-drop-off days would be the last time I would see my mother alive and fully conscious. If I had known what was to happen, maybe I would have actually cared about something other than the dope. Maybe I would've held her and told her how much I loved her and how sorry I was for everything I had done. Maybe. But maybe not; if I am being honest, the drugs had such a hold on me by that point that I don't know if I was physically or mentally capable of thinking about anything other than my next high. I was so incredibly lost.

You don't think about stuff like that when you are young, like the fact that you might be seeing someone for the last time, especially when you're on drugs. I'm sure we said we loved one another because we always did after I was in the car accident years earlier, but I really can't remember for sure. You never know when it's going to be the last time you see somebody alive, so take advantage of every moment you have with your loved ones.

If I remember the date correctly, on October 18, 2004, my momma went to sleep and never woke up. Nanny told me that, according to the autopsy, Momma died from chronic obstructive pulmonary disease (COPD). However, anyone who knows anything about COPD, or any other lung disease for that matter, knows you don't just up and die unless something significant happens beforehand, like an illness or a worsening of the degree of COPD the person has. My mom was not sick and had never been on oxygen or anything like that for breathing. I know in my heart that she overdosed. COPD may technically have been what caused her lungs and heart to be so weak, but I don't think she would have ever passed like that if she had not have been using drugs. I have never actually seen the autopsy report. It is possible that it said that Momma died of a drug overdose, and Nanny just didn't want to tell me. Maybe she thought it would be a softer blow if it was just a physical problem and not something tied to our dysfunctional lifestyle. I'm not really sure, and it is not something I have really looked into. Honestly, it's something I would much rather forget ever happened.

According to Lee, Momma just lay down in the middle of the day and didn't wake up, but I knew her routine. She would party for days and crash. She didn't just take naps during the day unless she had been up partying. I don't believe she overdosed on purpose because she still had two different types of nerve pills left in her prescription bottles (which I ended up with). I know from her past attempts at suicide that, had she been intentionally trying to take her own life, she would have taken every pill she had. It happened twice when I was younger. Both times, it was all-or-nothing, with not a single pill left in her bottles. This was an accidental overdose, in my opinion.

Luke, my ex, came to Bear's house to tell me that Momma was in a coma. I was out somewhere partying. When I got back to Bear's, I found out what had happened to my mom, but I wouldn't leave. My momma was lying somewhere in a hospital bed in a coma, and I wouldn't go see her. I guess I couldn't deal with it. I must have been thinking, Out of sight, out of mind. Or, maybe I thought that if I stayed there and stayed high enough, then it wasn't really happening, and it would just go away. I called Nanny to check on Momma every day. When they moved Momma to Vanderbilt University Hospital in Nashville and called for all the family to come in, Nanny, Nick, and Lee came to Bear's place, picked me up, and took me to Nashville, which was about one hundred miles away. Now, I *had* to deal with it. I couldn't run anymore.

At that point, Momma had been in a coma for four days. When we got there, I found out that there wasn't any brain activity. That was the real reason that we had been called in—for the administrative task of deciding whether or not to turn off Momma's ventilator—but Nanny didn't tell me that until we got there. They left it up to me to make the decision whether to turn off the machines that were artificially keeping Momma alive. I was in my early twenties and was, legally, her next of kin, or at least on equal footing with Nanny, who wanted me to be the one to decide. When I gave my consent, they turned off Momma's ventilator, and I stood there watching, hoping she would breathe on her own, but she didn't. She couldn't. She was gone.

I laid on her, crying for a few minutes, just holding onto her. I couldn't believe my momma was gone. The only person who had ever truly loved me unconditionally, no matter what I had done, was now gone. I was crushed, but I was also numb. It was like I had a switch. I felt that enormous rush of pain for a minute, and then I just turned my emotions off. I had become cold and hardened. I asked the nurses for a piece of her hair and her armband with her name on it, and I left.

If I had not been high when I got to the hospital that day, I think it would have been really hard for me to follow what I knew Momma's wishes would have been. She had told me exactly what she wanted to happen in just such a situation several months back, not long after my own overdose. She and I had been sitting in her living room snorting

Neurontin and smoking pot (because that's all we had at the time), and she started talking to me about how she was having chest pains. She said that the doctor had told her that it was just anxiety. She said, "Amanda, you know I have had anxiety attacks since you were a little girl, and this is not anxiety." I knew she was right. I was well aware of her anxiety attacks; I could remember her having them off and on since I was very young. She then began to tell me that she never wanted to be a vegetable because that was no kind of life and that she wanted to be cremated because the Bible says, "Ashes to ashes and dust to dust." She also said that she wanted her ashes spread over Monterey Lake. It's like she knew her time here on earth was almost over. At the time, I didn't pay much attention to it. Honestly, considering how messed up I was at the time, it's surprising that I even remembered our conversation, but I did. Immediately, when I saw her in the hospital room lying there lifeless, it all flooded back to me, and I did exactly as she had asked.

Nanny, Nick, and Lee went on out to the vehicle. I went to the gift shop and got busted for trying to shoplift. I know you have to be thinking, *Your mom just died, and you go straight to the gift shop and start stealing?* That is how bad my addiction had gotten. I had to have a release of some kind in order to escape those feelings, and stealing was the only escape I saw.

For some people, especially those who struggle with addiction like me, stealing gives them an adrenaline rush very similar to getting high on meth. I managed to run out of the hospital, and Lee picked me up on the side of the road. I'm not sure how he found me. Nashville is a big city, and that is a very crowded part of town. Now, I see it was God. If I had gone to jail and tasted a little bit of reality, I don't think I could have handled it. I believe I would have had a nervous breakdown, a mental collapse of the sort from which I may never have been able to recover. Lee got us out of town as quickly as he could, and we were soon on our way back to Monterey.

• • •

Remember that selfless prayer that I told you Momma had prayed when I overdosed? She asked God to save me that night, even if it meant taking her. That prayer had been answered. Momma was gone, and I was still living. Seven months after Momma prayed that selfless prayer as I lay near death myself, she passed away. However, her death was only part of the answer; the rest—the part of me having a life like she had, with marriage and children—was still to be answered. It didn't happen immediately.

Soon after Momma passed, I got into more trouble for stealing at Sally's Beauty Supply and Fashion Bug. That was ironic, I know, because I couldn't have cared less what I looked like at that point, but I just had to steal something, and that was the most convenient place to go at the time because it was next to Walmart. I was charged with two counts of misdemeanor theft, theft under $500, and one count of evading arrest for trying to run again. I was taken to jail. Lee and some of my friends came immediately and bailed me out. It was just a miracle that they didn't find out I was wanted in another county for violation of probation and send me directly there, but that wasn't God's plan. It was only one county over, so it had to be God who kept them from realizing I was already wanted because that just doesn't happen, not normally, anyway.

I never went to court over those charges. I just continued to run and stay in other counties. I never stayed at one place long. I was afraid to stay anywhere too long.

Chapter Twenty-Five

Divine Protection

I was an absolute mess, a bona fide mess. My mother had just died from a probable drug overdose, I was on the run from the law, and I was a strung-out, drug-addicted needle addict… and I wasn't even twenty-four years old yet. My life was miserable. Things had been bad before Momma's death, but they were definitely worse afterward. Perhaps reflecting what was going on with me personally, my car was in such bad shape from all the wrecks I had been in that the headlights were tied on with plastic zip ties and wire. If I hit a bump or went down an old dirt road, which I did a lot, then I would have to get out of the vehicle and adjust my lights because they would point straight up to the sky.

Maybe my headlights were trying to tell me something about where to find the help I so desperately needed: I had to look up to the heavens. It was probably no coincidence that those little beams that were supposed to guide my way pointed straight up every time I hit a bump in the road. The answer to all the "bumps in the road" in my life was up, to Jesus! "Lift up your heads for your redemption draweth nigh" (Luke 21:28, KJV). As obvious as it seems now, I didn't figure it out for a while. Actually, it might be more accurate to say that I didn't *give myself over to it* for a while; on some level, I knew that there was no way that I could pull myself out of the mess I had made of my life on my own.

I had many accidents while driving, but the scariest wreck I remember happened when I was coming around "dead man's curve" on Clarkrange Highway. I nodded off and woke up to a semi-truck blowing its horn at me. I clipped the guardrail on the opposite side of the road; the trucker had to go on my side of the road to keep from hitting me. There were so many times God protected me that I can't even begin to remember them all, but this was by far the scariest one that happened when I was behind the wheel.

Not only was my pitiful little car falling apart, *I* was falling apart. I wasn't just a mess on the outside; I was an even worse mess on the inside—a train wreck. A literal and figurative disaster, looking for a place to happen. After Momma's death, I had begun to mix all kinds of drugs together, along with alcohol, just to try to get high and escape the pain I was feeling. It didn't matter what kind of crazy controlled substance cocktail I threw together or even how much of it I took; however, I couldn't escape the pain anymore. The drug-induced numbness that I had sought as a means of escape for more than a decade was no longer there. Try as I might (and believe me, I did), I could not escape the mental torment and turmoil that my life had become. The drugs and alcohol that I had always used in order to escape from reality simply did not work anymore.

Let me backtrack for a minute. Undeniably, I started out using drugs as a pre-teen because I thought it was "fun" and the "cool" thing to do; however, it didn't take long for me to realize that the drugs gave me the peace that I craved in my life at that time. They helped me escape from all the trauma and issues from my dysfunctional childhood (as well as whatever current problems I had in my life). For years, that's what drugs were—a form of escape—but now they didn't work anymore. There was no more escape. There was no more running. I couldn't run from myself or from my problems anymore. I couldn't numb everything out like I had for so long.

I was a twenty-three-year-old needle addict, a child of divorce, now half-orphaned. I had no job, very little education past high school, not much work experience, no stable living arrangements, and had to stop and tie my headlights back on right every time I hit a bump in the road. Like those lights, I was hanging on by a thread. I was miserable, absolutely miserable. If you look in a thesaurus to find words similar to misery, you will find a checklist of my life on a daily basis during that time: unhappy, distressed, wretched, hardship, suffering, afflicted, anguished, anxious, angst, tormented, tortured, agony, pain... hell. Check, check, and check; I was living in every single one of those.

It wasn't just my mother's death or my own state of addiction; it was cumulative trauma. In addition to everything that had gone wrong during my childhood and teenage years, I was now also tormented by everything that had happened between Momma and me after I had become an addict. The fights. The physical abuse. The codependent, dysfunctional way that we fed off of one another when we were at our worst. I had been numb and had little or no conscience for so long that, when I finally began to feel and process emotions again, I was in absolute torment.

At the time, I had no idea that what I was feeling, finally *feeling*, was the conviction of the Lord. I didn't even know what that meant at the time. A "conviction" (in the legal sense) for drug possession or shoplifting, that was a concept that I understood. Being convicted meant that I had been found guilty in a court of law and had to pay for my wrongs by serving time, paying a fine, or reporting to a probation officer. This new kind of conviction—in which the Holy Spirit was pulling at my heart—was completely new to me.

My dad had recently given his life to the Lord. He had married Jannie, a good, Christian, Holy Ghost-filled woman who truly loved God, loved my father, and loved me. They were all praying for me up in Virginia. My aunt Linda, Jannie's sister, spoke to Daddy and told him not to worry about me because I was "coming in," meaning I was "coming into the fold" by giving my life and heart to the Lord. That would certainly have been news to me had they shared that information with me at the time. Back in Monterey, I was going about life as usual, with no idea that people were praying for me or that I was under conviction from God. The good Lord was working on me, the most wretched of sinners, and I didn't have a clue.

I didn't know it, but Momma's prayer was being answered. She made a lot of mistakes in her life, but my mother always believed in the Lord. She never got to experience His healing power here on earth, but I do believe she has gotten to experience it on the other side. Thank God for His grace! I believe with everything in me that He gave her time to repent, that He gave her a chance to make things right. I remember the last Easter that she was alive; we went to a local church there in Monterey. Momma went up front, and she cried and prayed with the pastor. I didn't understand what she was doing or why she was doing it at the time, but I do now. She was making peace with God while she still had the time. I am so grateful that I have that memory.

In the months after Momma's death, my addiction continued to get worse. My life, in general, deteriorated to a new low. For many years, my days and nights had revolved around getting high (a horrible existence in and of itself), but now my mother was gone, and I was on the run from the law. Both of these things made life so much harder. In truth, Momma had always been my enabler. She took care of things, so I could focus on getting and staying high. After she died, I was completely on my own for the first time. No longer would Momma swoop in and save the day with pot, pills, and money; now, I was solely responsible for finding my own food and shelter—and drugs. I didn't have Momma there anymore to run to in order to have those needs, wants, and desires met.

In spite of all the mistakes we both made, and all of the bad memories I have concerning my mom, one of my last memories of her is the most important. In praying over me when I was going through the overdose a few months before her own death—by putting her faith and trust in God and turning the course of her life over to Him—Momma was showing me what to do. She may not even have realized it; in fact, she probably didn't (Honestly, it's not like she had worked particularly hard to be "a good example" for me up until that point. Her prayer was both selfless and selfish; she didn't want to go on with her own life with the pain of having lost her child to a drug overdose. As a mother myself now, I can understand that).

After Momma died, I remembered her prayer, regardless of her motivations or intent at the time. I knew that she hadn't just spoken some empty words into the air. She had displayed a faith that there was someone above who could hear her words and who had the power to answer her plea. Because my momma had prayed over me as I lay there, close to death from a drug overdose, I knew that I, too, could pray, that prayer was always there as a possible option no matter how dire the situation. I knew, firsthand, that there was power in it. I might not have openly admitted it at the time, but somewhere inside, I knew that I was the walking embodiment of the power of prayer. Even though I did not yet have a relationship with Him, I believed that there was a God and that I could pray to Him if I got in a really bad spot.

After losing my mom, there were times when things got so bad that I thought I was dying. I can remember praying to God that I wouldn't die, even though, deep down, I didn't know whether I really wanted to live or not. I remember opening up cans of peas to eat with nothing else. I remember eating nothing but pancakes for a week or longer because that's all we had. That happened while I was on the run and staying with a lady in an old cinder block building on the outskirts of Monterey. Ironically, the building had once belonged to my grandpa Oden. He had operated it as a bar and hotel, back when he had killed the man who had threatened him. According to things I have read since then, Grandpa Oden had gone up on the roof and was waiting for the man when he got there, having been tipped off that he was on his way.

Needless to say, the local cops were very familiar with the location and my family's connection to it. They came looking for me there. Some of the guys who stayed there had already shown me where to hide if the cops ever came. When that inevitable event happened, I scurried up into the attic and hid as best I could, just like I had been told to do. I can still remember clinging to the rafters in that cold, cinder block building when the officers got there. I was so high on meth and cocaine that I was a pulsating, nervous wreck from the speed and the fear.

My body was literally vibrating from head to toe as the cops shined their flashlights up in the attic. I even saw one officer pop his head up through the attic door. It was just by the grace of God that I was not caught that day. Again, it was not God's will for me to go to jail. Don't misunderstand; I do believe that going to jail is God's plan for some people. I know of more than one person whom the Lord miraculously saved and delivered while that person was incarcerated. God not only used them greatly while they were in jail but even more so after they were released by sending them back into the jails to be witnesses for Him and to testify as to what He can do in the lives of those who put their faith and trust in Him. However, for reasons that only He knows, it was not God's plan for me to be behind bars.

• • •

The first time that I can say for sure that the Lord was drawing me into Him was one night when I was driving around with a guy who had been drinking. Even though I had been up and high on meth for days, I guess we figured that I was more alert than him and, thus, better able to drive. However, I was most definitely not sober. As we were driving down the road, I was telling him about losing my aunt, my mom, and my little cousin. All of the sudden, I felt something run through me from the top of my head to the soles of my feet. I actually said to him, out loud, "I just felt the Holy Ghost from the top of my head to the soles of my feet!" He probably thought that it was just an expression, or maybe he just thought that I was crazy, but I had just had the first encounter with God, who was getting ready to radically change my life.

Just as a side note, at that time, I had no idea what the Holy Ghost was, let alone what the Holy Ghost felt like. This was God Almighty coming upon me and speaking through me, but I did not know that. I wish I could tell you that I fully surrendered to the Lord at that time, but that's not what happened. I honestly didn't understand what was going on, so I just went on with life as usual. As bizarre as it probably seems, after that encounter with God, I just went back to my drug dealer's house, got even higher, went with him to a motel room, watched him pass out, stole some of his dope while he was asleep, and got high again.

While the dealer was asleep in the hotel room, after getting high, I called my stepmom, Jannie, to talk about the Holy Ghost. Crazy, I know. Most people who are Christians and who have never done drugs or lived this kind of life probably think I am crazy right about now. It's hard to understand the process, but, see, I didn't know anything about how God worked. All I knew was that I had felt something that I had never felt before and that words had come out of my mouth about a "Holy Ghost" that I didn't at all understand. The only thing I knew to do was to contact the one person who not only loved me in spite of me but also knew all about this Holy Ghost that I was now so curious about.

Thank God, He loves us right where we are, but He loves us too much to leave us that way. Some people might say that there is no way that God could or would visit someone in that kind of shape, high as a kite and strung out, nearly out of their mind, but I can assure you that there is no way I could be telling you this story right now if He had not visited me right there, right then, right smack dab in the middle of my mess.

Jannie tried to explain to me what had happened. I didn't really understand, but I knew I liked it, and it was exciting. Nothing had been that exciting or intriguing like that to me in years. Even though I was curious and intrigued, it wasn't enough to pull me away from the drugs quite yet. I remained in Tennessee, but I did keep in touch with Daddy and Jannie. They wanted me to come to Virginia and stay with them. I agreed, finally, but then I kept putting them off. I didn't want to leave my dope, my dealers, or my drug life. I just couldn't. I didn't know how.

Finally, we set a date and a place to meet so that I could go to their home for Christmas. The night before I was supposed to leave, I wrecked my car. I really believe that it was God's will; He knew that if I had that car (even with its many dents and its pitiful, dangling headlights), I would have just kept running. By then, I had been running for so long that I didn't even know what I was running from anymore. Of course, technically, I was running from the law, but, even more so, I was running from me—from the life that I had created for myself, as well as from all of the hurt, pain, trauma, and embarrassment. I know now that if I had a car, I would've postponed the trip again… and again… and again. I would not have left the drug world because I could not cope with my life without dope. I didn't know how.

There was an ice storm that night. I was paranoid and tripping, as usual, seeing things that were not there, or so I thought. I thought there were black things, almost like people but in what I thought were solid black full-body suits from head to toe, chasing me down the road going as fast as my car. I don't know what I thought they were at the time, but now I think they could have been demons or maybe even death itself coming to take me. While this was happening, I went around a curve driving way too fast, still looking around at whatever was behind me. There was a bridge that I was supposed to drive over, but I missed the bridge and headed straight toward the river. As I came to the end of the embankment, while looking over into the river, I saw a huge hand come down and stop me. The hand was as big as the front of my car. At the time, again, I thought I was tripping and still seeing stuff, but now I know it was the hand of Almighty God. He saved me. It was as if He said, "Oh no. This one is mine. I have heard the prayers and the cries of her loved ones, and I'm bringing her in." I believe God had my number, so to speak. I know He heard my momma's prayers and knew that my family in Virginia was praying for me, too. I also believe that He had an ordained plan for my life and knew that, as soon as He could get me in the right place spiritually, mentally, emotionally, and physically, I would fully surrender my life to Him. That night, however, I still wasn't quite there.

My car was stuck in the embankment, but I was able to get out. I speed-walked, almost ran, to my dealer's house, which was located not far from where I wrecked. He had a tow truck/ rollback. He and a friend of his tried to pull my car out but were unable to. My car was completely stuck, deeply mired into the mud and muck of the riverbank. They said that I was one lucky girl and that they didn't see how I had done that. Now I know, that's because I hadn't done it—God had.

They got my stuff out of the car and took the tags off, so the cops wouldn't know it was me. We sat at my dealer's house and watched as the cops and the wrecker drove by a little while later. We had a police scanner, so we were able to listen to them talk about my car and the wreck. They said the driver was "unidentified," and that was exactly what we wanted to hear. Of course, the cops could have looked at the VIN number on the car and used that to trace the owner of the car, but they didn't. Once again, here was another little piece of the puzzle of God's plan. Jail wasn't my intended destination.

• • •

The next morning, a friend took me to meet my dad. It was two days before Christmas: December 23, 2004, to be exact. I was officially on my way back to Virginia, the one place where I had previously been able to maintain at least a relative degree of sobriety, short-lived though it had been. Unlike the first couple of times that I had gone there—when I still had some ambition left—I had no hopes, no dreams, no expectations. All I had at that point was an overwhelming sense of desperation. My mother was gone, my car was gone, and I couldn't even walk down the street in my hometown without fear of being put in jail for violating probation.

My uncle Sam (from my stepmom's family) came with my dad to get me. Uncle Sam, too, had once been a drug addict. He knew what I was and where I was in my addiction. He turned around in the car, looked me straight in the eye, and told me that I was going to a place where a lot of people loved me. I have never forgotten those words, even though I was high when he said them to me. At the time, I thought to myself, *These people may think that they love me, but they don't even know me. If they really knew me, they surely would not, or could not, love me.*

Deep in my heart, I thought that I was a completely lost cause and not worth the breath I was taking in. I thought that Uncle Sam was crazy and/or was just trying to be nice to me, but his words still stuck with me. They resonated deep in my soul. They were words that I desperately needed to hear at that moment. I needed someone to love me. *Me.* Not the cute young girl I once was, not the co-dependent, enabling, verbally and sometimes physically abusive drug addict that I had become in most of my friendships and relationships with men. Just me, the person that I really was underneath the incredibly thick and complex veneer that I had worked so hard to build between me and the world.

In truth, I had lost my ability to love. I did not feel love for anyone anymore; I just used people and moved on, taking what I could get without remorse. Because I could not show or feel love toward others, I thought that I could never really be loved again either. I felt like the only person who ever really loved me was gone. There was never any doubt in my mind that my mother, incredibly flawed and broken though she was, had loved me. Every day of my life until the day that she died, I felt that love. It was the one thing that I thought I could always depend on. But that had been a lie; mothers die. I couldn't see how anyone else could ever really love me, not like she had. At that time in my life, I lacked the capacity to love and to accept love. I had lost all sense of love, but God put people in my life to show me love until I could learn to love myself and receive love from Him and from others.

As I left Tennessee and traveled to Virginia that day, I left more in the rearview mirror than I could ever have imagined at the time. I left behind the girl I had been. Oh, the remnants of her were still there with me, but they were fading fast. I just didn't recognize it for what it was. I thought the feeling of the Holy Ghost coming upon me had been the effects of a drug I was on; I thought I was hallucinating when God's hand stopped my car from going down the embankment and plunging me to my death in a deep, cold river. I saw things in the only terms that I knew at the time. For over a decade—more than half of my life—I had been a hardcore drug addict. That defined my world, and it was hard for me to see anything else.

Up until then, my life had been lived mostly as a wanderer, going from place to place and from person to person. All of my life, at least as far back as I could remember, I had been searching for that one elusive thing that I couldn't name but needed so very much. Whatever it was, I needed it as much as I needed the air that I breathed; I wasn't whole without it. For years, I had thought that drugs were the answer. I had convinced myself that it was a high that I was searching for. At least on a temporary basis, the meth, crack, coke, pot, pills, and alcohol had seemed to fill that place within me that, otherwise, felt so desperately empty. I was coming to realize, finally, after my momma had died and the drugs' effect on me had changed, that all I had been doing was numbing myself. I could chase the train every day of my life, but I would never catch it. It was only an illusion—a vapor, a ghost I had created in my own mind. It had never been real.

What was real, what truly did exist, was the hole that had been growing inside me since I had been a small child and my family had fallen apart. That hole, that void, was still very much there and, in fact, had become even deeper as I had grown from a little girl into a young woman. As a child, I had once longed for a relationship with my daddy, but when that had finally happened in my teen years, I had been too caught up in addiction to even notice. I loved my daddy, but it wasn't him that I needed. He was just a man, an earthly man who meant well but was far from perfect. What I needed was my Father. My heavenly Father. As I left Tennessee that day, the chasm within the depths of my soul had become so large that no person or thing or drug—not even the needle—could fill it. Only Almighty God could.

Chapter Twenty-Six

Amazing grace

Remember that desperate young woman that I described to you at the beginning of this book? The one who was in a car that was stopped by the police and who ran into the cold, dark woods to try to escape? The one who hunkered down under a log and prayed for a meaningful change in her life, as officers shined flashlights all around searching for her? It was just a few days after that when Momma died, and a couple of months later that I went to Virginia with nothing but the clothes on my back.

I left Tennessee on December 23, 2004, with one pair of shoes, one jacket, two outfits of clothing, and a few sleeping pills. That was all I had left to my name. I had no home, no vehicle... almost literally nothing but the clothes on my back, and even they were dirty and worn out, just like me. I had been stripped of everything materialistic and meaningful in my life. The materialistic things didn't matter nearly as much as the fact that my aunt and my mom were gone and my little cousin had been adopted by someone outside our family. I had lost everything and everyone who mattered to me, and I hated the person I had become: a lost, hopeless drug addict who was currently running from the police.

My first Christmas without Momma was a blur. I didn't feel much of anything. I was dead inside. I was emotionally numb. I sat at my dad's Christmas dinner in an emotional fog with a blank stare. I was coming down from the high that I had been on for so long, and reality was settling in. As much as I fought not to believe it or acknowledge it, Momma, Aunt Sissy, and Daisy were all really gone from my life. As long as I had stayed high, I remained somewhat numb, and I didn't have to face reality. I didn't have to feel anything. As long as I didn't feel, I didn't have to deal with reality. I had been on meth and other drugs for so long it was like I was living another life, a life in another world, a world I had created, where only what I wanted to see and deal with was there.

I slept off and on for the first week or so that I was in Virginia. As long as I slept, the withdrawals didn't bother me too much. When I was awake, I wanted to numb out so bad. I didn't want to feel what I was starting to feel. I tried to reconnect with some of my old drug connections in Virginia, but (by the grace of God, I now realize) I couldn't reach anyone. I did manage to get a little weed from my cousin around New Year's Day. By this time, I was starting to stay awake and feel more, so I started taking more sleeping pills and smoking pot to numb out. However, my supply was very limited when I got to Virginia, and what I had was running out fast. My mother wouldn't be showing up at the door with a fresh supply of marijuana and nerve pills "to keep me from getting sick" while I attempted to detox this time.

About the time I ran out of weed, I got the bright idea to go to the dentist and get a tooth pulled. I knew I could get some pain pills if I did this. In truth, my tooth really was broken and hurting pretty bad, but my primary motivation was to get dope of some kind, any kind. I went to the dentist and had my tooth pulled as planned, and the dentist gave me Lortab (an opioid painkiller containing hydrocodone). I went to my dad's and snorted all the pills within a few hours. I got so sick. It was nasty. I had never gotten sick like that from Lortab before, in spite of having taken it many times over the years. I thought that maybe I got sick because I hadn't used any pills in a while. I'm sure that was part of the reason, but now I know there was more to it than that. I had a lot of people praying for me, that same "Holy Ghost" I had felt while driving had begun to work on me, and I didn't even know it.

My uncle Tim, who had been in recovery from drug addiction for many years, had been asking me to go to recovery meetings with him. I kept telling him that I wanted to go, but when it was time to go, I would always make excuses and tell him I'd go next time. The last time he asked me to go was the day I had gone to the dentist. I was kind of high and kind of sick. Once again, I made an excuse not to go, telling him that I couldn't attend the meeting because my mouth was hurting.

I didn't know it at the time, but Uncle Tim told Daddy and Jannie that same day that he wasn't going to ask me to go anymore. The next day, after I puked my guts out and couldn't enjoy the high from the Lortab, I was calling him and asking him when they were having another one of those meetings. I went to my first recovery meeting while actually sober, with my uncle Tim, on Wednesday, January 5, 2005.

The next night, I went to church with Daddy and Jannie. A young guy, close to my age, came to preach. I believe God sent him specifically for me. I didn't know anyone even close to my age who lived that kind of clean and holy life. I was even thinking to myself, What are you doing in church? I thought he should've been out partying or at a bar like everyone else I knew in our age group. I thought that's just what you did. All the people I knew lived the same kind of life that I did, the drug life, the party life. I wasn't around any "good people" my age who were living right at that time.

The young man preached a really good message that night, and I felt something that I had never felt before, but I still didn't know what it was. Some people, including that young preacher, were saying, "Conviction's here, conviction's here!" Two of my cousins even asked me to go to the altar—I guess everyone except me knew what was going on—but I said no. I didn't know what conviction was and had no idea why they thought I needed to go to the altar or what I was supposed to do if I did go down there. They were all correct; however, the conviction power was there. I felt convicted for every bad thing I had ever done to anyone, especially the things that had happened between my momma and me.

When I went home that night, I prayed and got saved, right there in my bedroom at my daddy's house. There was no preacher, no altar, no choir singing me down the aisle. It was just me, alone in a little bedroom provided by my earthly father, finally ready to receive the power and spirit of my heavenly Father, Almighty God. It was the most awesome, supernatural, spiritual experience I have ever had. I had a true divine visitation. It may seem hard to believe, but I know it to be true.

At first, I wondered if I was tripping from years of heavy drug use. Then, I thought maybe it was some strange variation of withdrawals from all the drugs. Pretty soon, I figured out that what was happening to me was no hallucination at all. It was real. It was so real. I was lying in my bed all alone, or so I thought. I began to pray and bawl like a baby. I was hurting so bad inside. I lay there crying, praying, and asking God to forgive me for all the awful things I had ever done to anyone, especially to my momma.

Right then and there, after I asked God for forgiveness, I felt the most awesome presence all around me. I was in a pitch-dark room, but

I saw lighted figures floating over me. I felt love and comfort like I had never experienced in my entire life. I felt peace, like I had been in search of for many years. It was like God Almighty Himself had come down and surrounded me with His love and comfort. I have never felt anything quite like that again, but I don't need to. I know that's what I will experience when I get to heaven someday. That one night with the King was enough to change the course of my life forever.

At that very moment, I was delivered! Does that mean I never again thought about drugs or battled this old sinful flesh? No, it doesn't mean that, but something miraculous had just happened inside of me. I was free. I was really set free. No one had to touch me except the Lord God Almighty! He knew what I needed. He knew I needed deliverance from the demons that were controlling my life, and when I was completely yielded to Him, He did the work!

In active addiction, I had done things that I didn't even want to do, and I had gone places I didn't even want to go because I was so bound by a power greater than myself: the demon of addiction. It controlled me. I was a puppet, and the devil was the puppet master. For years, I had been led to places I didn't want to go and kept me there longer than I wanted to stay, but, praise God, the enemy no longer controls this vessel!

• • •

The next day, I called my ex-fiancé, Jamie. It happened to be his birthday, and we hadn't talked or laid eyes on one another in over two years. I figured he would hate me because of the way that things had ended between us and that he might not even be willing to speak to me. As it turned out, however, Jamie was heading in my direction that weekend to look at some tires for his truck. He agreed to stop by

Daddy's house and pick me up so that I could go with him. I got him a birthday card and made him a homemade chicken pot pie for his birthday.

In the card, I told him how sorry I was for everything I had done to him. I also told him I understood if he couldn't forgive me, but I just needed a friend. I felt he was the only one who could really understand what I was going through and how I was feeling because he knew how much my momma had meant to me. The "friend" thing immediately went right out the window. We had only been in each other's presence for a short time until I was lying in his lap, crying like a baby over my momma. It hurt so bad, and I didn't know what to do or how to feel. Over the next few days, we dealt with a lot of emotional issues from the past that were not easy at all to face.

The first night we were together, Jamie and I both drank some alcoholic beverages. Like I said earlier, the flesh still wanted to be sinful in some areas, even though my spirit had been transformed. At that time, Jamie was not saved, and I was brand new at this whole salvation-and-holiness thing. I only took a couple of sips that first night, but then, the next night, I flipped out and realized I couldn't drink anymore *at all*. Jamie had looked at my drink and mentioned how much alcohol it had in it, and I started flipping out, saying, "Oh no, I can't drink that. I'll get that same euphoric feeling. Then, I'll start wanting more, and the alcohol won't be enough. I'll go from alcohol to smoking dope, then snorting pills, then to shooting dope. That's the way it works." I poured my drink down the sink that night, and I have never drunk another drop of alcohol since then, nor have I smoked, swallowed, snorted, or shot up with any kind of illegal substance.

I had learned from the recovery meetings that alcohol is a drug. At first, I thought, *I'm not an alcoholic. I can drink a little.* Then, my conscience and the Holy Spirit kicked in and let me know different. Jamie still drank a little after that, but I didn't. I did take some sleeping pills once. I was a manic crazy mess. I ran around and talked like a madwoman and couldn't sleep. I went for, like, seven days with eleven hours of sleep. I was driving myself and everyone around me crazy. So, I took sleeping pills to knock myself out. I felt so guilty for taking the sleeping pills that I couldn't even sleep. I waited up all night for Jamie to get home from work and had him flush the rest of the pills down the toilet.

Something had changed inside of me. I had experienced a real encounter with God, and I would never be the same. I couldn't use anything, not even alcohol or sleeping pills (which I had been given since childhood), with a clear conscience. I had never realized how bad drugs were before. I know that probably sounds crazy, but you have to remember that I had been part of the drug world for the majority of my life, and almost everyone that I knew was also part of that world—not just my friends but also my mother, aunt, uncle, and even my grandmother. They all got through life with the help of some kind of "crutch," whether it was alcohol, weed, dope, or pills. Yes, I had been miserable near the end of my time as an addict, but I had never really felt bad about taking drugs. I did feel bad for some of the things I had done while on drugs (and to get drugs), but I had never felt guilty about taking the drugs.

The only way for me to explain it is to say that there had been a true change in my heart; something deep inside my soul had shifted, and things would never go back to the way they were before. From that night in my bedroom at Daddy's house forward, I felt the conviction of the Holy Spirit any time that I did something that went against God's Word. This was totally new. This was very strange. For the first time in so long, I actually had a conscience and wanted to do the right thing. When the Lord delivered me and saved me that night, something broke inside of me. The dam that had been holding me back from feeling the pain in my life had come crashing down. My emotions came back. I had a conscience again. The "real me" started to come forth. Not only did I feel again, but I wanted to make all my wrongs right. I started to love again. I started to live again.

The next time I went to church, one of my cousins on my daddy's side sang a song called "The Long Black Train." The songwriter was telling everyone not to go riding on that long black train, but he wasn't talking about a diesel locomotive. He was using "train" as a metaphor for sin (much as my friends in the drug world had used the phrase "chasing the train" in a figurative sense). I had been riding that long black train of sin for many years, and I understood exactly what he was talking about.

Thank God I had finally jumped off that train before I died and went straight to hell. The devil thought he had me, but boy was he wrong. I had been saved, sanctified, set free, filled with the Holy Ghost, and washed in the precious blood of the Lamb. The devil had tried to make me believe that he would destroy me through my addiction, that I couldn't escape, and that there was no way out. The devil is a liar and the father of lies (John 8:44). I officially became completely clean and sober on January 11, 2005. Since that day, I have never drunk another drop of alcohol or abused another drug.

Chapter Twenty-Seven

The Abundant Life

The thief does not come except to steal, and to kill, and to destroy. I have come that they may have life, and that they may have it more abundantly.

John 10:10

Although I had been saved, delivered, and set my heart and mind to serve the Lord, the enemy, the thief, the devil didn't want to let go quite so easily. I would be lying if I said it was all a bed of roses because it was not. It was not all easy, but God was faithful to be with me every step of the way as the thief continued to attempt to steal, kill, and destroy me. Eight days into my sobriety, I was diagnosed with Hepatitis C. I was devastated. I thought I had cleaned up for nothing—that I was going to die and that, even if I didn't die, I would never be able to have children. After getting the diagnosis, one of my first thoughts was to just get high and forget about it, but I didn't. Instead, I went straight to church and cried out to Jesus. I also kept going to recovery meetings and church, and I didn't use drugs, even though I really wanted to at times. Instead, I talked to some other people from the meetings who had gone through the same thing. I was told that if I did my part and did not use drugs, God would do the rest.

My new friends were right. The next time I went to the doctor, I was given a clean bill of health—no treatment, no medicine, merely the healing power of Jesus Christ. The specialist looked at my blood work and said she wasn't sure if I had actually had Hepatitis C. I told her I had been an intravenous drug user for years, and she agreed then that I probably did have Hepatitis C, but she couldn't explain what had happened. I knew what happened. Jesus happened. Even though I had given myself the disease, He had mercy on me and healed me. God is still in the miracle-working business; I am living proof!!!

After I was healed from Hepatitis C, Jamie and I decided to get married and start a family. Our beautiful, healthy baby boy was born on December 20, 2005. My precious little "Christmas present" was born five days before Christmas! It had been just one short year since I had arrived in Virginia as a broken-down, strung-out drug addict with no hope. Now, here I was, a healthy, happy, Christian woman with a loving husband and a beautiful, brand new son. How could I have asked for anything else? I had already been given the best present ever.

What a miraculous year that was! The year before, I had lost almost everything of importance in my life, but when I gave it all to God, He gave me more than I could ever have asked for, more than I could have ever imagined. I had lost my mom, my aunt, and my little cousin, but I had gained a loving, faithful husband (Jamie was saved a little over a year after I was) and a beautiful, healthy child. I had lost the most important person in my life, but through her death, I found life. I accepted Jesus, and He gave me not just life but life more abundantly (John 10:10). I now have the good life my momma prayed I would have, only it is so much better than Momma could have dreamed of—a man who truly loves me, freedom from the bonds of drug use, and the many blessings of a life in service to God. I never knew this kind of life was possible, especially for someone like me.

Many years have now passed since my momma prayed over me

as I lay dying from a drug overdose. The sick, terrified, addicted girl who finally cried out to God from under a pile of logs in a cow pasture a few weeks later has been transformed, by the Holy Spirit and the grace of God, into someone that girl would not have even recognized back then. I have a wonderful life today: a strong, Christ-centered marriage, not just one but two beautiful children, my health, many friends, and a wonderful "stepmom" who is really my "God-mom" who has loved me unconditionally and shown me the right way to live. I also enjoyed a healthy relationship with my earthly father until his passing in December 2020.

Like I mentioned at the beginning of this chapter, not all days have been dancing through the tulips and daisies. There have been some struggles, including losing my father-in-law Jim ("Blow Bag") to addiction and suicide, my uncle Nick to a drug overdose, my half-brother Kevin to addiction and suicide, and my dad most recently, just a few short months ago. I would be lying if I said I had not thought about getting high multiple times during these losses. I did have those thoughts from time to time. Of course I did. I also dealt with anxiety, depression, grief, trauma, and even thoughts of ending my own life a few times. I was able to survive and thrive all these years because of one thing, and one thing only (and it certainly wasn't my own willpower). Of all the blessings in my life since I got sober, I am most thankful for that number one, most important relationship in my life, and that is Jesus Christ, my loving Higher Power.

I am also thankful He has put wonderful people in my life along the way and has taught me how to make it through tough times. He never promised us it would all be easy, but He did promise us that we would never be alone. During early recovery, I learned not only to run to God and His Word but to trust the people He placed in my life. If it had not been for my dad and stepmom, Bill and Jannie, my sponsor, Donna, and my husband, Jamie, there are many times I am not sure I would have made it. I know how to read. I know how to pray. I know how to get "a word" from God, but sometimes we just need to be in His presence more than anything and feel His love more than anything else. God has allowed me to feel that at times, just me and Him; other times, it has been when He has shown His love to me through others.

My husband Jamie

My sons Evan and Caleb and our baby dog Lucky.

My God-given Mama Jannie

I am most definitely an advocate for not only a relationship with God but a strong relationship with people. This is the very foundation of the Ten Commandments from which the twelve steps of recovery are derived. I found strong relationships not only in my family and church but also in recovery meetings. The recovery meetings helped me understand why I did what I did. My weaknesses, my trauma, my motivations… It was not enough for me to know I was forgiven and be set free. I needed to work through steps to let go of years of shame and guilt, so I could understand why I was the way I was in order to heal. This is still an ongoing process, to be very honest. I have also sought professional as well as Christian counseling over the years. I even went to college to become a counselor myself (yes, I eventually finished my bachelor's degree—and went on to get my master's, as well, and currently working on my licensure! God's grace is most definitely sufficient!!!) I highly recommend counseling, not just because I am a counselor but because of how greatly it has impacted my life. The Bible tells us there is wisdom in the multitude of counsel. Many times, others can see our blind spots where we cannot.

• • •

Going back to when I was first saved, coming out of addiction, and developing a relationship with this God I wasn't so sure about, there was a period of adjustment as I went from being a "little baby Christian" into a mature follower of Christ. Even though I most definitely knew He was real, and I knew Jesus died for me, and I accepted Him as my Savior, I had a lot of questions. Part of it had to do with my own worthiness, but after I began to feel and accept His love and understand the sacrifice that Jesus made to atone for my sins, there was something else that I had to know. *How could a loving, caring God have allowed* me to go through so much in my life—all of the dysfunction, pain, and turmoil that I experienced as a child and young adult? Why did He allow those things to happen to me? I knew He loved me, but I still didn't know how I was supposed to turn my life over to Him and trust Him to take care of me. Everyone I had trusted in the past (including my parents, who were supposed to love me the most) had hurt me in some way. Over time, God helped me realize that *He* never hurt me but, instead, had actually protected me many times, both from myself and from others. Yes, things had been bad at times, but they could have been so much worse. We have been given free will. People make choices. I had made many bad choices, and others in my life had made bad choices. It was those choices, whether mine or someone else's, that had hurt me—not God.

Let me say that again: *God never caused anything bad to happen to me in my life.* It was just life, lived out in a fallen world. Bad things happen. The devil uses these things to try to destroy us, but I know a God who can take all of the pain, hurt, heartache, guilt, and shame and use it for His glory and your honor. His Word says that He can give you double honor for your former shame and give you beauty for your ashes (Isaiah 61). His Word is true. He has given me honor where I had shame. He has given me beauty where all I had left was ashes. When I was finally willing to give Him my ashes, He gave me something much more beautiful than I could have ever created on my own or ever even imagined.

In due time, He even miraculously set me free from all my legal charges in both states. Whom the Son sets free, is free indeed (John 8:36). He truly is a Miracle Worker! I never spent one night in jail after being saved. That was only by the hand of the Almighty God. I've said it before, and I'll say it again, God is still in the miracle-working business!

Epilogue

Now, as I finish writing this in the year 2021, it has been over sixteen years since I gave my heart to the Lord. God has done many miraculous things and brought me through many trials in my life that I plan to share more in detail at a later time in a future book. To make a very long story short, my husband is now saved. We have two boys, ages nine and fifteen. They are beautiful children who love the Lord and know nothing other than serving the Lord. My husband and I have both become ministers inside our home church as well as at other churches and media outlets. I am also the founder and president of Healing in the Hills, a substance abuse community coalition. If anyone had told me I would be the president of anything, I would have laughed, but, again, God is still in the miracle-working business!

God has recently called my husband and me to pastor our home church, Open Door Ministry Revival Center. That is our current number one assignment from the Lord outside our home, which is always our first ministry. God, family, then ministry outside the home. Priorities are of the utmost importance, and ministry always starts at home.

God is no respecter of persons. What He has done in my life and my family's life, He can and will do in yours if you let Him. The details may be somewhat different, but the storyline is always the same: from death to life, from destruction to restoration, from brokenness to wholeness. Whatever the enemy has tried to kill and destroy in your life, whether it is spiritual, mental, emotional, physical, or a combination of these, Jesus can bring life. He is "the Resurrection and the Life" (John 11:25).

"But I want you to know, brethren, that the things which happened to me have actually turned out for the furtherance of the gospel" (Philippians 1:12). "And we know that all things work together for good to those who love God, to those who are the called according to His purpose" (Romans 8:28). Today, I have the abundant life Jesus died to give me. I am a "new creation" in Him, and you can be too. "…Old things have passed away; behold ALL things have become new" (2 Corinthians 5:17).

Thank God, I made my journey From the Needle to the Cross. Will you make your journey today and accept Jesus Christ as your personal

Savior? It's simple. All you have to do is pray this prayer, "Thank You, Lord Jesus, for dying on the cross for my sins. I accept You as my Lord and Savior. Forgive me of my sins. Come into my heart and make me a new creature, in Jesus' name. Amen."

If you honestly and earnestly prayed that prayer and are willing to surrender your life to Him, you are now a completely new creature in Him, and you can start anew with a fresh walk and life with Him. Find a good, Bible-based church close to you and get involved in service work and reading God's Word. That is how you will truly begin to grow. If you are an addict, I also highly recommend that you seek professional help in the form of counseling, rehabilitation, or other community support services. You don't have to go it alone. God will be with you, and He will put others in your path to help you along your journey. You just have to take that first step of surrendering your life to Him.

• • •

Most of this book was about my life before I met Jesus and turned my life over to Him. I don't want anyone to think I am in any way glorifying that kind of life. However, telling my story as openly and honestly as I could was the only way I knew how to explain how God had kept me even through the hardest of times before I came to know Him.

Although writing this book has been painful, it has also been very therapeutic for me. I have had to look back at a lot of things that I would otherwise have kept buried in the past. However, my main purpose was not to help myself (and certainly not to glorify the lifestyle I once engaged in) but, rather, to be an encouragement to anyone out there who is currently suffering with addiction or who has suffered with addiction in the past. If that description fits you, I want you to know that you are not alone and that you do not have to let the guilt and shame of your life during active addiction haunt you anymore. Also, I wanted to give hope to the hopeless—those who may still be stuck in the vicious cycle and see no way out. There is a way out, and His name is Jesus! Don't give up! He loves you!

Lastly, I want to speak to those who have loved ones who are lost to drugs and alcohol: don't give up on them, don't quit praying for them, and never quit loving them. I don't mean that you should condone or enable their behavior, but do let them know that you love them no matter what and that you will be there when they get ready to get help. Miracles do still happen today. I am living proof. Every day of my life is a miracle from God Himself!

Anyone interested in booking, upcoming events, or resources for substance abuse treatment you can contact me by e-mail at FromTheNeedleToTheCross@gmail.com.

CPSIA information can be obtained
at www.ICGtesting.com
Printed in the USA
JSHW041954300622
27470JS00006B/10